Dermot Nelson

These Things I Imagine

(A collection of plays and poems)

PLAYS

'Changes, through Their Eyes'

Nurse working in Methadone Clinic

Hi I'm Claire, I've been working here at the Community Drugs Team outreach centre the past four years now... Now I know what you thinking... "What is an attractive girl like me doing working in a place like this" Well the truth is I want to be here.... I'm helping people.....I'm helping people who want to help themselves..... Was I scared when I started? Oh God Ye!! I was expecting to see Freddie Krueger look-a-likes and gangs of hooded skeletons or decrepit looking desperate people prostrating themselves on to their knees in front of a doctor begging and pleading with him to just sort them out with a fix.......But it wasn't like that....There were healthy looking people....some a bit pale, and some very thin and some did look very malnourished...but they were human...they didn't look nearly as menacing as I'd imagined.... and what's more, they were nice.... not just to each other...they were nice to me...a normal person......They asked about each other....about how they were keeping and how their families were getting on....And they smiled when they heard something good was happening in each other's lives...They were human, loving humans...And they grew on me.

Sick people trying to get better, trying to get their lives back....Sometimes it was very upsetting...like when you see an 18 year old child coming in and they're so down and out....they think this is going to be their life forever.....or when you see a middle aged patient who feels they've already lost everything and have just given up.......but it can be a great laugh too ye know, the banter and the slagging matches between the patients....and the workers.....And sometimes it can even be uplifting...like when someone realises that this doesn't have to be it for them, and they find hope....or an x-patient calls in to tell you they've got a job or are back in education.....or they've been re-united with their kids or their family....or even when they just come to visit and you can see how well their doing....It just makes it all worthwhile....and I feel grateful for having been a part of their recovery.......But sometimes people die...and its soul destroying....then when the tears are shed, it leaves me determined to make sure my

6

other patients don't go that far....determined to do what I can to help them stop using.

You know it's easy to label or to throw stones at people when you're not directly affected by the issues that they are dealing with....For some people the eye opener is when a particular social problem seems to follow them home, ye know starts to happen in their house.....For me it was when I realised I wasn't working with demon junkies...I was working with people...Sick, sad people.....People who I could really help...And people who could really use it.

I started here four years ago...six months work experience while I was training to be a nurse...And I've never left....in four years I'll still be here...or in some other clinic, helping some other sick people who don't want to be sick anymore.

Middle aged man

How does she work there...a nice girl like that....how does anyone work there for that matter...those people....I can't stand the fact that I've to work on the same street as that place.....Mind you, we petitioned against it...but we couldn't gather enough signatures...all the business owners signed but very few of the locals....Well I suppose that's to be expected, half their kids are probably patients there.

What kind of parents let their kids end up like that....do they not know what their kids are up to, or do they just not care....probably on it themselves...wouldn't be surprised, not when ye see the age of some them junkies..... I can't even stand walking past them...ye just know when they look at you their thinking "how can I rob this fucker"....Thank God I don't live in the city and my kids aren't exposed to this... We've a nice four bedroom house in the suburbs...me, my wife, my son and my daughter...it's nothing to fancy but it's comfortable.....and we don't have to see the likes of them outside our window.....mind you, they're not too far away, or at least people like them...You know what I mean...people from those estates...you know the ones, the ones that are like entering the untamed wilderness, only instead of meeting tribal people your met by groups of youths, and in place of war paint and spears they've got hoodies and bottles...gangs of little animals...and their parents are no better....and we're expected to accept them in our shops and places of business knowing they're there to steal something or cause some kind of annoyance.....and I'll never understand why the government don't get them buses and schools of their own where they can't infect decent kids with their hash and their E tablets......Well at least I know they'll never turn my kids....mine are great , the kind of kids you don't have to worry about.

Danny 15 year old boy

Alright! I'm Danny.....some people call me the Rocket....there's no stopping me, captain of the football team two years running and God knows how many times I got man of the match....See Me Da....the big lad.... he's alright, kind of set in his ways but he's alright. Gives me a few pound on the sly every now and again, ye know when we win a match or I'm going to a disco or whatever....He's always like "don't tell your mother , she already thinks you get too much"....Lets me have the odd couple of cans too...ye know at Christmas and birthdays and that...He's cool that way.....But he's not always cool....he doesn't like some of my friends, or some lads I go to school with....He doesn't even know them! "Watch that family" he'd say or "don't be seen with him" or "ye know the way that lot behave" or his best one yet "they're a different breed".....There from a different fucking estate! Like, if you walk a few blocks and cross a green your there! I think my Dad expects there to be checkpoints on the entrance ...ye know like keep the riff-raff from mingling with us decent folk.....But he's not alone....they're all like that.....his friends....my neighbours....even a lot of my teachers.....But when we win a match, then they change their tune...some great little footballers over there ye see....and if their on our team then "they're a credit to the community".........Don't get me wrong, there are some heads over there I'd rather not know but it still isn't right....My little sister having her first proper birthday party, friends from school and all that, and she's told she can't bring certain kids from her class (*In a woman's voice*) "Them! In my kitchen! Oh I just don't think I could cope with that" How's she supposed to explain that to her mates (*In a child's voice*)"sorry you can't come to my party my mummy's afraid you might spit on the new carpet, or carry some new breed of head lice" I could be over exaggerating slightly but ye get my point.

Ah, the little sister now she's a character....she's always floating around the house in tutu's or princess gowns or fairy outfits....she got annoyed with me the other day, I was walking through the sitting room and I saw she was playing, waving this plastic stick around so I said "Oh no a wicked fairy, Please don't turn me into a frog" well you want to have seen the look she gave (*In a child's voice*) "IM NOT A FAIRY, IM A PRINCESS" I was like "oh, soorrrreey" some kids take their playing very serious ye know.... a sceptre, a wand? I'm a teenage boy for fuck sake, how am I supposed to know the difference...I have more important things on my mind (*Next line said in a daze*)...like...breasts...and how to get to see them....and more importantly, how to get to touch them.

(*Snapping out of it*) And money......me and the lads started smoking a bit of spliff lately.....we wanna start getting 50 bags....we were just buying 10 bags off a fella in school but he got caught ripping another lad off....he had no smoke so he was selling him an Oxo cube as hash and a teacher walked up...caught red handed... he was expelled...(*next line said in* astonishment) they couldn't do him for dealing so they done him for fraud.......I know smoking its illegal, but it's not really that bad....just a few smokes at the weekend......it's not like we're junkies or anything.

Girl who's x- boyfriend was an addict

Don't talk about smoking; I'd love to have a wee spiff.... I can't though.... I couldn't bring myself to.... I know it's not the same but it brings back too many memories of my ex-boyfriend... he was strung out... Him and his mates just sitting around the house all day... all glassy-eyed and goofing off their heads.... He's off it now... and I know he's getting his head together, but I couldn't get back with him, not now... It just wouldn't be the same......When we started going out he was so much fun....so full of life... His energy seemed to light up the room...and he made everyone feel like his best friend.... he was so cheeky too....at family occasions if he wasn't dancing with my mother he was chatting up one of my aunties....But that all changed.... As addiction took over he seemed to become more and more of a recluse.... only leaving the house to score or go to the shop....he became shy and withdrawn, and seemed nervous in public.... And he got so thin....it was painful to look at but it was worse when he was sick from withdrawals... He tried to go cold turkey a few times...it was horrible, lying in a foetal position on the couch or on the floor....muscle's tensed, head aching, stomach cramps, diaorreah and vomiting....and if you heard him! Pleading with God to take away the pain.....to free him off his addiction...promising to be a better person....but it didn't happen.....Sometimes I thought maybe I should just buy him some gear... and end his torment.....but I didn't.....and in the end he always gave in himself.....Cold turkey just wasn't the way for him....... I wish I could have stayed with him...but I couldn't...... I could never forget the images of him that way..... and I felt let down by him....there was one time when he was in recovery and I was sick, really sick, and I was worried about it....and I felt I couldn't even tell him because of the state he was in....It was a really hard phase of his recovery and I didn't think he could deal with my stuff and his.....It didn't seem fair....I'd been there for him! And I wanted him there for me.... but he wasn't.... and it hurt....... I told myself it wasn't his fault, but then I thought, "Well whose fault is it?" I hope he does well for himself....I think he deserves it... and I know he'll never go back to that life....well I hope he wouldn't.....I feel kind of guilty sometimes when I think about it.....we started to smoke gear together...... I was just able to stop....And when he was badly strung out and trying to quite....at his most vulnerable....sometimes I'd get frustrated and angry....or really upset, and I'd call him names, names I knew would crush him. Waster! Scumbag! Junkie!

But I didn't mean it.

Teenage Girl

(*Comes on shouting*) JUNKIE!   I HATE THAT WORD!   Words like that keep people down.... People like my brother....Sorry... I didn't mean to get so worked up....it's just ...you don't know what it's like having a brother who's an addict....like mine is....He's getting better now...he's nearly finished his methadone program...but he hasn't told my parents yet.... I don't blame him... but I still think he should.... he said it's going to be really hard and that's why he's left it for so long..... But I think the sooner the better... he could use their support.... He says he's waiting for the right time....but I know its shame and guilt holding him back...... And fear, afraid of their reaction....Afraid of being disowned....or cast out... Maybe he's right...I mean when you see how people react when they find out about him....I found out from some girls' in school... he was seen coming out of a clinic a few times by one of the girls sisters.....You should have heard how they told me.... Announcing it loud enough for the school to hear.... and the way they were talking about him.... They were saying all sorts....talking like he was a filthy animal....saying stuff like "Dirty Junkie" and "Scumbag!" Of course I lost it.... I didn't believe them... Bitches! ...I still had to ask him though... so I rang him... He said "No don't be silly"   But then he came to see me... and he told me that he was a recovering addict...and he was sorry I'd had to find out that way....sorry I'd had to hear it at all... His eyes were holding back the tears...And I told him it was okay... he put his head down like he was so ashamed...and that's when I cried...I'd never seen my brother put his head down in his life....and I didn't like it....I hugged him and he started to cry...then he started to laugh and he apologized for being such a pansy... We both kind of

14

laughed...and I asked how I could help... He told me just being me was enough...and then asked that I didn't tell anyone else till he was ready.... And to ignore the girls in school as best I could...... "Junkie, Scumbag" My brother was never any sort of scumbag.... He's always been a good person...and a great brother...even as a teenager when all he wanted was to be out with his friends... He still made time for me....he got down on the floor and played whatever I wanted.....He must have hated it...but he did it anyway because I was his baby sister...and he'll always be my big brother....Addict or not.

Mother of a recovering addict

When you bring a child into the world you never imagine you'll have to deal with this kind of thing....it doesn't cross your mind that your new baby, a brand new life could one day be a drug addict....And why would it? The thought is so horrifying you'd probably want to keep your baby inside you forever where you know that they'll be safe....but you don't ....you have the baby....and you're overwhelmed at their beauty, in awe at their sheer tininess, and amazed by their utter helplessness....they are one hundred per-cent dependent....dependent on you...and it feels magical.........And you watch them grow their whole lives and its beautiful.......from a stinky baby.....to a noisy infant....to a hyper child....to a moody teenager.....to an ungrateful adult.....and they're still precious to you.....all you want is the best for them....and you will do what it takes to protect them.....But you can't always be there...you can't always know what they're doing....and when they get in trouble...real trouble...you begin to question yourself.....Is this somehow my fault?.... Did I not do enough to protect him?...How did I not see this coming?....Am I a bad mother?......You batter yourself with a barrage of questions that are eating away at ye........Then you get angry.....angry with yourself, angry with your child.....angry with God.....you begin to question Him.....Why my son?....why mine?....is it something I've done?....What could I possibly have done to deserve this?...What could he have done?.......But when you see your child...you realise you have to put all your hurt and personal anguish aside....and you've to come to the aid of your son..........I'll never forget him coming home...he knew that we knew....his sister had let it slip.... He came in the back door and I looked at him....I was raging, wanted to kill him, wanted to go ballistic....he stood at the door with his head down and I said "Well?....Have you nothing to say?" He just started to stutter "I'm...I'm...I'm" my husband who'd brought him home said "Sarah Please" and he ushered him over to a chair beside me.........Its then that all my anger and hurt began to melt away.....and concern and compassion began to take over......His eyes were welled up.....he seemed to have a lump in his throat that made it difficult for him to speak....he was extremely nervous...I could tell by his breathing.... every time he attempted speech he started hyperventilating....so I lifted his head to look at his face.....I was shocked by what I saw.....He looked so frightened...so alone...so full of pain....My heart broke!.....this wasn't how I wanted to see my baby boy......so torn...so broken...so full of guilt and shame......I took him in my arms held him in close to me and told him not to talk....all that matters now is my son has come home.....that's when he really cried....he wailed uncontrollably.......I wondered what terrible things he had seen? Had he been through?   We stayed like that for hours...and all I kept thinking was my precious little boy what have you done to yourself.....and in my head and in my heart I was promising him that we'd fix it....that we'd get through it together.

When I think of it I should of known he'd get in some kind of trouble.....when he was a young fella he was always up to something.....he was so bright...so bubbly.....everybody loved him....but he was a little rogue.....I'll never forget him in primary school......I used to do a good bit of baking years ago...and I remember at one stage it seemed to be vanishing very fast......I couldn't for the life of me figure out how.....At the time there were only the three of us in the house........well it turns out he was selling buns and slices of gurcake to the boys in school who got lunch money.............And that's not the half of it......a few years later he started hanging around with this fella whose parents were both teachers in the secondary school....the kind of fella who had the latest of everything straight away.... we couldn't figure it out...that wouldn't attract our son....and he was a lot quieter then the lads he usually palled around with.....Well, Ye wouldn't believe the shock I got when his principle rang and said that himself and young Smith had been producing and selling pornographic magazines!...for the few months previous they had been collecting page three's and little clips and cut outs from everywhere and anywhere they could find them....and had been blowing them up and photocopying in the office in Mr and Mrs Smith's house, then stapling them together and selling them as magazines!...they had a weekly issue... that's when the unlikely friendship made a whole lot more sense... Of course my husband thought this was hilarious...not only that, he was proud of him..."he's going to be an entrepreneur, a business mastermind" was what he said....I wanted to punish him...he wanted to get him a present.

When I think about the trouble and the mess he got into as an adult I wonder if I knew him at all as a teenager.....God only knows what he got up to in secondary school....he probably just got better at hiding things.....he definitely got better at hiding things....I should have noticed a change in him though.....I did at some stage, and I knew he was losing weight... but I never imagined....Sometimes I want to ask him questions about stuff....but I rarely do....I think I'm afraid of what the answer might be................It's funny when you realise your own are no angels you kind of feel guilty about how you've treated others.....not physically or even verbally....but about how you judged them without even knowing them....and you want to apologise.....but what would you say....your kind of humbled and you find you've compassion toward people where you wouldn't have had before....you develop a new tolerance and understanding, a tolerance and understanding that you wish everyone could share.

Former Addict

Tolerance and understanding...we like to think we have these qualities....but sometimes I'm not so sure..... I used to see people who looked a certain way and think...Waster...Scumbag...Junkie....I felt nothing for them but distaste or disgust, and for some reason would associate them with being dirty or filthy.....As I got older I changed....my mind opened....unfortunately not by wisdom, in fact probably by lack of....my mind opened through life experience........I went through a dark patch in my life....three and a half years ...struggling between addiction and recovery...... three and a half years...wasting my life.....three and a half years...rotting the very core of being......three and a half years... ignoring my God given right for something better.

There's no way to put in words what it feels like to be strung out.......raw...harsh...desperate....when you're sick from withdrawals you can feel it in every part of your body.....and your mind!.....every minute is more unbearable then the last...it's like a momentum that keeps building and building and building...but just never reaches its peak....it gets worse and worse, builds and builds, more and more.... and you just want it to end....even just for a minute….but it just won't stop.... and you consider doing terrible, horrible things...things you'd never do...just to end the torment.... only a split second thought.... and then you feel hours of endless guilt for having thought at all about doing such vile acts.......Finally ye manage to borrow some money...or steal something....or ye sell something...so ye go out and score....and as your using the horrible sickness and the head fuck seem to fade away...and for little while, while a wave of relief is washing through your system....your almost able to block out the pain of your miserable existence.......but it's never really gone....it's always there in the back of your mind "I'll never beat this" "It has me for life" like as though your future was set in stone.....and you hate yourself.......Sometimes the anxiety and the desperation would get so bad that you'd just want to end it.........but you know you can't.....for your parents sake.....for your little sisters sake......for your girlfriends sake.......Then you get angry......Angry with God......Angry with God for letting you become this.....this, this junkie!......then ye get angry with yourself, cause you know it's not Gods fault.........but ye struggle on.........I struggled on....

I tried cold turkey a few times....it wasn't for me.....it beat me every time....and every time I felt more defeated, more downhearted and more shattered....eventually I did what every addict wants to do but can't find the strength to.....what everyone in trouble or in pain should do......I asked for help......I went to an outreach centre and I started a methadone program.....ye see it's hard to ask for help, for anyone!...and it's hard to say "I am an addict" it's painful to say.....painful to know......But it's the first step on the road to recovery......and I feel Blessed that I took it.......Unfortunately not everyone does....and it's sad....or some go on the molly and never come off it......I can't help but feel sorry for them....and I wonder how they feel inside...how they are in their heads.......I still drop by the clinic now and again...to see how people are....and say hello....and I'm delighted when I hear someone's after getting clean....so happy for them....and I think it really encourages others........ I still see the same snobby fucks coming in and out of the offices and shops near the clinic...I'll never forget the way they'd look at me as I was coming out of the place....like I was nothing....less than nothing....a piece of shit....and I just knew what they'd be thinking "would ye look at this junkie fucker...probably thinking about how he can rob me" ....fucking twerps!!

But I got better...and I'm doing good now...and my parents are proud of me for getting off it...proud of me....imagine...I just feel ashamed for doing it in the first place....all the people I hurt....and it's not like I can say I didn't know what I was doing.....I can't justify it in my own head let alone try and explain to somebody else....I just know that I did it and I don't anymore....

Il never forget my first time going home when my parents found out...I was near the end of my programme....I was already very emotional and I really didn't know what to expect....my nerves were that bad I was finding it hard to breathe....My father collected me from the bus stop....he didn't say much on the way home....don't think he knew what to say....I walked in the back door and looked at my mother.... she looked angry....I put my head down...I began to think it was a mistake coming home....when she spoke I could hear the anger in her voice... I couldn't look up to meet her gaze....I was finding it hard to speak...I had a lump in my throat and I was stuttering.....my father spoke to her gently and then guided me across the kitchen to the chair beside her....we were sitting there a couple of seconds in silence....but it seemed to last a life time....I could feel goose bumps all over my body...and my lip was quivering...my heart was palpitating.....I tried to speak but could find no words....as I trembled....there in front of my parents......eye's cast down.....still battling with speech...my mother raised my chin with her hand and looked at me....I could sense a change in her as she stared into my eyes.....I began to cry.....with loving hands she wiped the tears from my face....and slowly her eyes began to water....as I watched the tears run singularly down her cheek I again attempted to speak....but couldn't grasp a word....she took me in her arms and said "sssh don't speak my son is home that's all that matters" the tears erupted from my eyes and she pulled me in close to her.....I was like an infant who'd been hurt clinging to their mother..... I cried and cried....I was overwhelmed with emotion....and even when I couldn't cry anymore...probably because I was close to dehydration....I still sat there in her arms... I felt so safe....so warm...so loved.....we stayed like that for ages....and finally when we loosened our grip and the feeling came back into our upper bodies...my father told me "We can fix this....You no longer have to do it alone"....he looked kind of injured as he spoke...and he asked why I'd left it so long to tell anyone....why I hadn't told him....then he said something which I will always remember "do ye not realise son, I'd walk to the ends of the earth for ye" and I'll never forget the look on his face as he said it....he seemed to be hurt by the fact that I'd gone through so much alone.....or maybe.....it was that I just didn't grasp the depth of his love for me.....Afterwards it felt great....I felt immeasurable relief....I felt accepted.... I felt I belonged... it was beautiful....it still is.....I thought I'd lost it....but I hadn't.....it was me that was lost.

I'm not saying it was easy after that...but it was easier....I didn't feel so alone anymore.....you could have all the people in the world around you and still feel alone if you try and deal with things by yourself.....For a long time I had a girlfriend...but at some stage she'd had enough....and for a while I couldn't understand....why wait till someone's nearly better to leave them....but now I think she'd probably taken all she could....maybe for my sake she'd been waiting till I was better to end it...and just couldn't wait anymore....or maybe, she'd found something better....it's hard to know....I don't blame her though....I can only imagine what it must be like... to see someone you love, like that...in that condition.......it must have taken unbelievable strength.......And it must have worn her down so much.

Ye see I believed I was a junkie and a waster.....and when you believe you are something it's hard to get it into your head that you're not....or that you can stop being......Even months after I had finished my methadone programme every time I took a shower I told myself I was washing away another little bit of the junkie....till finally one day I didn't need to anymore....there was no more junkie....because I didn't feel like one anymore....and no-one tried to make me.....that was the when my life started again.....and I began to look forward.....But sometimes I look back.....and I think of all I've been through...and I just think where it all started....it's funny I thought I knew it all...when really I was so innocent.....I mean I used to be the rocket....there was no stopping me...captain of the football team two years running and God knows how many times I got man of the match.

THE END

BY DERMOT NELSON, 2011

In The Clear

(The play begins with a group of teenage boys sitting around telling stories. One boy holds the groups attention as he recalls a story of a bloody encounter.)

D=Decky A=Adam AE=Alter Ego B=Boy etc

Decky: The lads held him down while my dad punched his head in; and when he was done, he left him to the boys, they broke both his arms, and all his ribs, he was fucking mangled by the time they were finished!

Danny: Nice one!

D: Fucking right, he wasn't down our way again in a hurry, nor was his scumbag mates!

(The lads all smile and nod in approval)

D: It's not like that anymore, in them days their position meant something, now they can't even defend their community with people shouting their mouths off. Nothing's changed Peace my bollocks.

(Adam comes on stage)

D: Where were you?

Adam: Having dinner with my family!

D: Faggot!

A: Ha at least I get fed ye skinny fuck!

D: SKINNY, you mean healthy, just because
        you're a fucking porker!

A: HEALTHY, you're like an albino Ethiopian.

*(The boys start mess fighting; Decky gets Adam in head
        lock and wrestles him to the ground)*

D: Not too skinny to take you though, am I?

A: Let me up!

D: Say 'I am a faggot and you are the king,
        and I'll let you up'.

A: You're a faggot and I am the king!

(Decky squeezes harder)

D: Oh cheeky! Say it properly now don't have
        me make a fool of you in front of all your
        friends!

A: Okay okay, I'm a faggot and you're the
        king!

(Decky lets him up and the boys all laugh)

A: Ye wanker! I should have held my ground; I can tell I almost had you in the crushing grip of reason.

D: Aye you did alright! You all set for Friday night; it's going to be epic!

A: Why what's on Friday night?

D: WHAT? Are you taking the piss?

A: Obviously mate! (In a London accent) I'm fuckin tooled up idinit blood!

D: Sweet, you remember what those wankers done to Vinnie last time?

Vinnie: Seven fucking stitches!

D: A rock to the head! See if I see the cunt that did it!

V: See if I see him myself! (Makes slit throat gesture with hand)

D: I wonder if 2 litre Peter will be there?

A: Who?

D: The boy Danny here bottled 2 litre bottles of cider over the head! Smash smash (makes motions with his hands, boys all laugh and cheer and clap Danny on the back)

A: Ye you mad fucker ha, but do you think maybe we can have a go at some wee girls this time, before it all kicks off like?

D: You need to get you're fucking priorities right Adam! Its fuckers like you end up getting done, wandering off with a wee girl next thing you're surrounded by them fuckers, those scumbags will show you no mercy, besides there's plenty of wee girls around here isn't there.

A: Awk I know but I want something different, there all the fucking same around here and everyone knows each other.

D: What do you mean DIFFERENT you want to be with one of them, Traitor!

A: That's not what I meant...

D: AND another thing! It's being the same and everyone knowing each other that has kept our community alive, and kept us strong in times of trouble, but you're too good for that now, are you? You're just like them fuckers in the estate that say they want change; they seem to forget all the travesties that happened here cause them cunts.

A: Awk that's not what I meant, I just meant I
        wanted to meet a new girl or two, not one
        of those ones, just someone new who
        doesn't know me as well as I know myself.

D: Well when you're ready to see sense again
        you'll realise that when you go mixing with
        outsiders it only leads to trouble, for
        everyone, this is where we were born and
        where we'll die, no-one gets in and no-one
        gets out, just the way it should be......and
        in case any of you ARE ever planning on
        mixing with the likes of them ones just you
        remember, traitors are not fucking
        tolerated!

A: Awk Decky don't be getting on like that,
        we've been best mates since we were five,
        Its always going to be me and you and
        don't you forget it, I just want a bit of whit-
        woo without the world fucking hearing
        about it is all!

D: Awk I know what you mean, but there will
        be plenty of other opportunities for that,
        we've got to get these fucks for what they
        done to Vinny and Smithy the time before
        that, and fuck knows how many others in
        the past, we have got to show them just
        like our dads did in their day, we are not to
        be fucked with!

Danny: Aye right enough well said man!

A: Ye, your dead right, scumbags!

(The lights go down over everyone on stage except for Adam, his Alter-ego steps up from the shadows)

Alter-ego: The way he talks about them, it's like they're not even human. Is that really what you think?

A: Ye, they're them and we're us………well, well no sometimes, sometimes I wonder, I can't really see… I can't see…. Awk I don't know….

AE: Don't know what? Can't see what?

A: I can't see the difference, flags, religion, title, all the killing, the hatred, I wonder if it's worth it!

AE: But yet you'll curse them anyway, call them names, fight them, and to what end?

A: I have to! I have to fit in, awk you know what the boys are like, what Deckys like!

AE: Blinded by hatred? Mind warped by tales of savage acts violence, some told to him as tales of glory? Are you going to let his hatred dominate you too?

A: What can I do?

AE: You can speak out! You can become a man and tell your friends what you really think!

A: Aye right, well if being a man means being a fool, than I'd rather stay a boy!

AE: So what? Are you going to raise your children here to? What if there are still Deckys knocking about, using peer pressure and loyalty as a leverage to make them do things they don't want to do? What if your kids are more easily influenced than you OR what if they fall for one of them, the others, gets mixed up with the 'enemy' what happens then?

A: That's years away, I'll be moved far away from here by then, my kids will be fine!

AE: This where we were born and where we'll die, no-one gets in and no-one gets out!

(Lights go down, when they come back up the stage is split into two rooms that resembles bedrooms, there is a teenage boy in one and a teenage girl in the other, they are getting ready to go out, girl is on phone to friend, when she hangs up the boy rings her)

Sam: I can't believe they let me go; I'm so excited I have butterflies and everything! *(Pause)* No, my mummy convinced dad to let me get the bus! *(Pause)* I know I'm so nervous, he said he wants to meet me at

7:30 and we'll get the bus together *(Pause)* Okay see you then, bye…

(Kyle looks in the mirror breaths deep and talks to himself, he is preparing to ring Sam)

Kyle: Okay, you can do this, it's simple, she likes you, and you like her, agghhh, why am I so nervous? Fuck it here goes!

(He picks up the phone and rings)

S: Hello!

K: *(speaks like Joey from friends)* Hey how u doin?

S: Pardon?

K: *(still speaking like Joey)* So eh whatcha wearin?

S: What?

K: I, I, I mean hi Sam, its Kyle!

S: Oh Kyle, I thought it was a prank call.

K: Ye, ye s,s,sorry about that I was, I was, it was, it was my b,b,brother he's always joking around with my phone!

S: Oh, well tell him I said *(mimics the accent) I'm doin fine* and I'm not telling him what

33

I'm wearing (*laughs, she knows it wasn't his brother*)

K: Ye I, I will later he's gone now! So how are you?

S: I'm great thanks, you?

K: I'm brilliant, I mean I don't think I'm brilliant, I mean I, I mean I feel brilliant

S: (*she laughs gently*) I know what you mean, relax Kyle!

K: (*he laughs nervously*) Okay, I'm sorry. Are you excited about tonight?

S: Ye, I can't believe I'm allowed to go!

K: I know! It's going to be epic; everyone is going to be there!

S: I don't care about everyone; I can't wait to see you!

K: I can't wait to see you either; this is going to be a night to remember!

(Lights go down and come upon half the stage with Adam in his bedroom getting ready to go out, Kung-Fu fighting is playing and he is singing along but the music goes down as the dialogue starts, looking in the mirror as he speaks)

A: Aye, there'll be Kung-Fu fighting alright
        *(Does some mock moves in the mirror,
        then as he says the next line he raps a belt
        around his hand)* we are coming prepared
        this time, no cunts catching us on the hop!

AE: Those dodgy fucks don't know what's
        coming for them!

(In American accents)

A: Damn straight!

AE: I can see it now; they won't even have a
        chance to start shit.

A: *(Normal accent)* No chance *(back to
        American)* we'll be on top of those
        motherfuckers!

AE: I can almost feel the blood squirt on to my
        face!

A: *(Normal accent, slightly surprised)* what?

AE: *(Normal accent)* as six of us kick one of
        them around the ground, kick his fucking
        teeth in, I don't his name but who cares I
        know I hate him!

A: I wouldn't go that far!

AE: NO? So how far would you go?

A: Just enough to show them, give them a
        fright!

AE: How far is far enough? How far is too
        much?

A: I don't know! They do it to us too!

AE: Oh, when is the last time you got a
        kicking?

A: I just want to be one of the lads; I just
        want to fit in!

AE: One of the lads, or one of the pack?

A: One of the lads! We like fighting! So what!
        Big deal! Everybody does it!

AE: Everybody doesn't do it, and not
        everybody wants to do it, you beat guys
        you don't know, guys who don't want to
        fight you… why?

A: I don't know, because it's a war!

AE: Oh, and you're the heroes? There's glory in
        it?

A: Yes there's glory in it! They're them were
        us, it's a fucking war!

AE: There's not...........there's no glory in it, there is certainly no glory in fighting someone who does not want to fight you! That's more like bullying or assault. And you say that they're them and we're us, but that's not what you really think, you can barely see a difference you're just going along with the crowd, hoping it doesn't get to serious, while your friend rattles on about the glory days. The glory days are over if they even existed, a lot of innocent people died needlessly, always for cause or protecting a people, and people prayed for an end to it. Well you're neither defending your people, or fighting for a cause, you're creating more violence! Violence that breaths hatred and hatred can only breaths hatred!

A: Why do I have to be different? Why do I have to change things?

AE: Because you know it's wrong, you don't have to change things, but you definitely don't have to make things worse!

(Adam grasps his hands in his head as he is getting vexed)

A: Look! I just want to have a good night!

AE: I know you feel that nervous tension, each time you're going out its getting worse......you could stay in tonight, not get involved, you don't need to go out!

A: But they'll think I'm a coward... or worse!

AE: A coward? Maybe you are, or you wouldn't always say yes, maybe if you weren't you'd speak your mind, you let things happen get involved in things you know are wrong. You'd have more of an excuse were you a sheep!

A: A sheep?

AE: At least a sheep follows blindly, almost unaware, but that's not you, is it? You know this isn't right. Let's say no! Let's stay in tonight!

A: Aye maybe you're right; I'll just tell them I couldn't go out! But what would I say?

AE: I'm staying in tonight boys! I don't want any part of this; I don't want to be a part of a problem that has destroyed countless families for generations! I don't want to hate or be hated anymore! I want something better for the next generation, so I am saying no, I am staying in tonight!

A: I can't say that! Maybe I'll just tell them I'm sick!

(Phone rings, it's Decky, lights come up on other half the stage or maybe off to one side, it's Decky and some others drinking)

A: Bout you big man?

D: Are you near right man, we're all waiting on you?

A: Well actually...

D: By the way I was only winding you up earlier, come down here quick mate, Vinnie's after robbing everything from his Da's liquor cabinet, he's fucked already, ye want to see the get up of him...

A: I'm not feeling great though...

D: Awk wise up, a few drinks and you'll be fine, a few wee girls are here as well ye might even score before we go out, fuck it sure I'll call up for you!!

(Adams dad walks in)

AD: All set to go out?

A: Yep

AD: Goodman, don't be home to late, pretty soon it will be your sister turn to by heading out and I don't want you setting a bad example.

A: Ye ye, I'll be home straight after the night club

(Lights go down and come up in the club the boys are standing in a group, some are dancing but Decky stands in the middle eye-balling everybody, one of his gang approaches)

B3:   Aye Decky, he's right there is at least one coach load of them here already!

D: *(Decky laughs and shakes his head)* Fucking Idiots!

B3:   We might be outnumbered!

D: *(Aggressively)* and what?

B3:   No, no, nothing I, I, I was just saying.

D: Well don't just say! And don't stutter either, ye sound like a fucking pansy! Right boys keep your eyes out for a target; wait until the end though, no point getting barred!

(Lights go down and come back up with an empty stage Sam and Kyle run on, they are panicking and as they are being chased, they stop centre stage)

S: What did he hit you for?

K: I don't know, but look it we can't keep
            running, we're getting lost, just go you and
            hide!

S: We'll both hide!

K: No they're gonna find us, it's only me they
            want, it will just be a few slaps and it will
            be over. Awk don't cry it will be okay just
            go and hide, they'll be here any second!

*(Sam hides at the side of the stage; the boys come on
            stage from back and side and make a wide
            circle around him pushing him about)*

Danny: Where's his bitch?

K: She kept running I couldn't keep up!

*(Decky hits Kyle a powerful blow and he's knocked to
            the ground)*

D: *(very sinister)* No-one told you to speak,
            the vile fucking lies your kind spout burn in
            our ears! Look about for her boys!

*(The boys look about but don't find her all the while
Decky just looks at Kyle menacingly; Kyle stares back
terrified as he slowly rises to his feet)*

K: She's gone I'm telling you!

V: Aye, she's not about

K: *(Kyle leans up as he says)* Look I'm sorry
            but I didn't do anything!

D: *(Decky floors him with another thump)*
            what were you just told? Are you deaf or
            are just stupid? Get on your feet? *(As he
            stands up the second time boys close in)*

B3:   Where are you from?

K: I'm from…

(As Kyle tries to answer Decky hits him again)

D: I've already told you twice about that
            haven't I?

*(Kyle just nods as tears and fear become more hard to
contain)*

D: Get up! Now what are you doing here?

*(Kyle says nothing and there is a pause, Vinnie smacks
him in the head)*

V: Answer him!

(Kyle looks around confused)

V: You deaf? He asked you a question!

*(Again Kyle looks around confused, looks in to the faces
of his assailants for help)*

B3:   What the fuck are you looking at me for?
        (Slaps him) I'm just waiting for my turn! So
        you gonna answer him or what?

D: Ye know I thought I asked him a question?
        Maybe I didn't!

B3:   Awk ye did Decky, ye did ask him a
        question!

D: Are you sure? Did I Adam, did I ask him a
        question!

A: You did aye, you asked him clear as day!

D: Why's he's not answering then!

A: Maybe he's something to hide?

D: Is that it, have you got something to hide?
        Something you should share with the
        group huh? *(Decky stares into his eyes)*
        What the fuck are you doing here?

K: *(Kyle is crying and stutters as he speaks)*
        I'm, I'm, I'm sorry please, I won't…

(Decky hits him a powerful punch and roars)

D: DO HIM!

*(Kyle falls to the ground and the boys are immediately
on top of him with a barrage of kicks and punches, as*

most of the boys continue the beating Adam and Decky step away adrenaline still pumping)

D: Some cunts just don't learn, do they!

A: No!

(Sam comes on stage crying)

S: PLEASE STOP!

(The boys back off Kyle who isn't moving or making noise anymore)

D: What have here?

S: Please leave him alone!

(Decky stares at her for a minute and then orders the boys off)

D: STOP, He's enough lads!

(The boys back off in a circle around the stage, she runs to Kyle crying and saying his name, Decky walks over and gently pulls her up by the arm, and speaks gently)

D: Awk he's okay, don't you worry. We just had to teach him a lesson!

S: A lesson for what? What did he do to you?

D: Fighting the wee lads the last time we were here, we can't let that go on now can we? What's your name?

S: What wee lads? Why'd you want to know my name?

D: He's always fighting wee lads every time he's here; we just had to put a stop to it. You probably missed your bus I could try and get you a way home!

S: I don't want a lift with you I want to go with Kyle!

D: Awk well get him home to!

S: *(In disbelief)* you'll get him a way home?

D: We done all we had to do, lesson learnt, isn't it *(looks at one of the boys and boy nods)* look there's no need cry, it's all over, we're hardly gonna leave you stuck out here are we?

(She looks at the Kyle and then turns away from Decky and takes her tries to take her phone from her bag)

S No, I'm going to phone help he's not moving

(He motions with his head for the boys to surround her; they do slowly like stalking cats. Decky comes up and gently takes hold of her bag)

D: He's fine he's only pretending because he's afraid we'll hit him again. We have a lift arranged; we can drop you both off.

(She notices all the boys around her and starts to walk back from decky slowly, he keeps hold of her bag and walks toward her)

S: I'll be fine, you can go now...........What are you doing, leave us alone, please, please, just leave me alone!

D: Relax we just want to help! (*He smiles menacingly at her*)

(As she tries to flee the boys play cat and mouse with her, she goes to leave in several different directions but they keep blocking her way out as they slowly move in, and she becomes hysterical)

D: We just want to know your name!

S: HELP KYLE! HELP

D: How's your boyfriend going to help, he can't even help himself.

(After a few seconds she can't escape Decky catches her from behind she twists and turns till she is facing him)

D: Now you get to see what a man feels like!

(As the lights fade out the boys are approaching and putting hands on her clothes, as it fades out completely Sam is heard crying and screaming NOOO before complete silence)

(When the lights come up the boys all run on stage out of breath but laughing clapping each other on the back)

Danny: That was fucking epic! What a hiding, he was knocked the fuck out!

V: Fuck the hiding ye faggot, what a ride!

B3:   Aye she was fucking sweet!

Danny: That little Kyle faggot wasn't doing much to stop us!

V: I doubt he'll be doing much for a long time!

(All laugh except Adam)

D: Say nothing to nobody! We meet back den at lunch time tomorrow, agreed?

A: What if we're asked why we're late?

D: You met a wee girl; you're not lying then are you?

(All laugh except Adam and as they all head off he stays and his Alter-ego appears)

AE: What have you done?

(Adam just stares)

AE: What have you been a part of?

A: It wasn't my fault, I mean, I, I, I couldn't have stopped it if I'd tried

AE: But you didn't, you didn't try! You were part of it!

A: I didn't know what I was doing, something just came over me!

AE: What? What came over you?

A: It was Decky, he's got some way of controlling you!

AE: Decky! Decky did what Decky did! Just as Adam did what Adam did!

A: Oh my God! What do I do now?

AE: WHAT DO YOU DO NOW? You get help and hope it's not too late.

A: I can't, who will I get? And the boys would think I was a tout!

AE: FUCK the boys; you've got to do something. Make an anonymous call.

A: What if they trace it, what if they find out it was me?

AE: That boy didn't move while you and your friends had your way with his girlfriend over and over and….

A: STOP!!! I can't think I just need to get home; I just need to get home.

AE: Get home and what?

A: And go to bed!

AE: Aye get some sleep it will all be okay tomorrow, except this isn't a dream Adam, this is really happening….If either of them die, THEIR blood will be FOREVER ON YOUR HANDS...

A: JUST STOP, LEAVE ME ALONE!! IM GOING HOME, I'm going home!

(The boys are all on stage except Adam like setting at the plays beginning, Decky is joyously recalling about the night before and Adam walks on stage stands back a bit and listens, he hasn't slept)

D: She was fit though!

Danny: Aye and I think she was loving it!

D: Aye right enough, I should have asked for her number   *(All laugh)*

D: I bet she'd of giving it too! Did you hear her moan? *(Does a moaning sound, they laugh again)* I wonder how her wee boy is feeling today, not too fresh I'll bet!

A: *(Adam speaks as sternly as he walks down stage)* her wee boy has severe brain damage, broken ribs and other injuries; he's in a critical condition!

D: What? Where'd you hear this?

A: It's in the paper!

D: It made the paper! Fuck, we should be fine; hundreds of people go to that night club. Does it give their names!

A: No it says he's too young to be named, and the only mention of the girl is that it was his and girlfriends first junior night club.

D: No way, wasn't she a lucky girl! It's not everyone gets a good seeing to their first night out!

A: YOU'RE FUCKIN DISGUSTING!

D: WHAT, have you got something to say?

A: YES, how can you joke and laugh about what happened, that boy could die and fuck knows what the girl is going through!

D: Are you forgetting you were there to? And you weren't complaining when you were tearing the clothes off her back, or when you were...

A: I KNOW...........But...but...I mean, what if she talks, the cops find out, our parents find out, jail?

D: I already told my Da.

A: What?

D: He was fucking delighted, said he wished he was there! He'd a given her turn and all.

V: Look Adam no-one's going to find out if we don't tell them, he can't talk and it doesn't look like she's saying much.

B3:   Even if she wanted to she doesn't know who we are.

D: Ye relax; my Da will provide alibies if we need it say he collected us or something. Besides I'm not sure she didn't want it!

A: What?

D: Well she wasn't crying for very long now was see!

B3:   Ye man, she was lookin bucked, did you not see what she was wearing?

D: Ye, and fuck her anyway, slag! She's one of them; not the same as us, so fuck her and fuck them, ye!

A: Ye...

(Lights go down on Adam, enters Alter-ego, through his speech Adam stares ahead)

AE: That's not really true is it? They sure sound the same to the rest of the world, they're born the same, they grow and play the same, ...they learn as we learn, age as we age, feel emotion as we feel emotion, happiness and sadness, anger and sorrow, suffering and loss...they breath the same, they bleed the same, and they cry out the same..... The difference is merely how we treat each other!

(Lights go down and come back with Decky and Adam in their rooms; Decky is getting ready to go out and rings Adam who is sitting staring silently at the floor)

A: Hello!

D: Bout you big lad?

A: Hey!

D: So did ye hear? The wee bitch committed suicide!

A: I heard!

D: You don't sound to fucking happy!

A: What have I to be happy about?

D: The other guy is goosed, he can't say a
           word

A: What's your fuckin point Decky?

D: MATE! WE'RE IN THE CLEAR!

*(Adam just drops the phone as Decky keeps talking and
           the lights go down)*

D: Did you hear me? Adam? We're in the
           clear!

*(As Decky is saying in the clear we here Kyle pleading
and voices saying "Shut up", "Their different" and Sam
crying and screaming out "NOOO", and the boys voices
saying "My turn, hold her" and the sound of hysterical
screaming and crying, his father's voice saying "your
sisters turn next" and voices filled with venom saying
they're not the same, this all fades away till it's just the
lines "we're in the clear" and the lights fade down)*

THE END

BY DERMOT NELSON, 2012

𝕽𝖆𝖇𝖚

Act One

(The play begins with a knocking sound; Rabu is on a rostrum up stage, where there are some big double doors, when he answer, in comes a cold but frantic Marie)

Rabu: Marie! So late, what takes you here? Come in and warm yourself, my dear.

Marie: Forgive me please about the hour. I pray your mood, it will not sour. I know that you must think me queer, this date, this hour arriving here. There's things in you I must confide, though in the morning I'm to be a bride. But all my thoughts are bent on you, I must know if you feel it too?

Rabu: Marie you mustn't! Do not persist. For love of you I can't resist. Thoughts of you they cloud my mind, no peace, no solace, no rest I find. I fight these feelings because it's wrong, when to another your hand belongs.

Marie: No Rabu! It's you who's wrong! My love for you is pure and strong. And though I do feel Peters love, to just make do is not enough. When you look at me I feel weak, I hang on every word you speak. It's more than childlike infatuation, with each passing glance comes captivation. My dreams take me to a sinful place, with you alone locked in embrace.

(She pauses, then describes dream in a daze gradually getting more excited)

Marie: At first there seems to be just me, then out of the darkness does walk thee. I get excited as we meet, my heart; it seems to skip a beat. I try to hide this, I feel so shy, your eyes can read me, and my face can't lie.

I try to talk and act so tough; you ask me, "Must thou treat me rough". As your stepping ever nearer, the truth in me comes ever clearer. My false persona is now breaking, you stand by me, my nerves, I'm shaking. I lose my breath, as you touch my face, my heart does beat at quickening pace. You look deep into my eyes, I tell you to stop but you know its lies.

I feel as though I'm powerless as you guide me to you, and then, we kiss! My lips they tingle, my limbs go numb; you caress my neck with your breath, lips and tongue. You seem to touch both soft and strong, it feels so right, it can't be wrong. I stop fighting, I can't pretend, and to you my body, I gladly lend. You undress us both right then and there, and hours of primal love we share.

(Pause then turn to face him)

This dream I have most every night, for now you see my souls in plight! Even daytime, my mind does roam, as I think of you in song or poem. I cannot take this any longer; my love for you gets ever stronger.

(She drops to her knees and wraps her arms around him; he puts his hand on her head)

You must take me this very night; do not reject me or die I might!
(He is comforting at the start of the line but his demeanour changes to nasty whilst he speaks)

Rabu: My dear Marie, take you I will, and in the morn your heart be still. No more anxiety or heart ache, your confusion and your pain I'll take.

(She looks up at him and leans back then slowly rises to her feet)

Marie: Though comforting words of love a token, there's something sinister in the words here spoken. In a moment your demeanour's changed, you look at me with eyes deranged. Who are you? Where's my Rabu? Those eyes, they don't belong to you! What's happening? You now seem bad, who are you? Am I going mad?

(He walks toward her slowly he has a smile on his face)

Rabu: I'm sorry, I really must explain. You mustn't think your gone insane. I am Rabu, the one you lust, the one whose eyes you love and trust. Only that's not all that I am, I'm more than that, than just mere man. I am a creature of the night, I fear only day and light. The last few months, your private hell, were only features of my spell. For that I'm sorry I'm told it's rude; one mustn't ever play with food.

Marie: Rabu stop you're playing, for me your scaring, I thought you more mature, more caring.

Rabu: Oh Marie, you know it's real, or do you doubt now what you feel? Am I everything you could wish, or do feelings for me still exist.

Marie: You are a demon of the night, a creature bent on human plight.

Rabu: Ha, I am no demon bent on plight but am a creature of the night. It's warm blood that I desire, from fair maidens I admire. And you Marie, I don't mind admitting you are ample, you're more than fitting.

Marie: Is there no other you could lure, it is not me you want, I'm sure!

Rabu: But I am sure and not mistaken, and you are ripe and for the taking. This is the reason why you're here, its time you met your fate I fear.

Marie: No please, please, it's not my time, on another maiden dine.

He walks toward her shaking his head and she steps back and continues to beg)

You couldn't have always been this beast, who longs for human flesh to feast?

He stops faces the audience and speaks as though thinking to himself)

Rabu: No I haven't always been this way, coveting blood, afraid of day. I was human I do recall, before I came to feel bloods call.

Marie: You must have had some family, imagine one of them were me!

Rabu: There are none left of my family line, on each of them, their blood, I dined!

Marie: You must possess some human feeling, are you content with life-blood stealing? No more lives you need to take, for I can end it all with wooden stake, and for your sins you can repent, your soul, my life blood need not be spent!

(Rabu says next line staring into space as if remembering and considering what she is saying, but he isn't)

Rabu: For so long now I've harvested blood. A release! *(Mockingly)* **impaled by wood? What you say now was said before, by me, when death was at my door. One hundred and fifty years ago, in a village that's name I no longer know. My father passed before he'd grown old, my family wintered hungry and cold. Being a boy of just nineteen, to be a man I was more than keen. Though I worked and lived at local mill, I could not support my family still.**

My mother and siblings, they would not starve, meat for them I'd hunt and carve. But by pain of death, hunting was banned, as greedy lords owned game and land. So I took to hunting by moonlight and being home by day and bright. For months it seemed the perfect crime, and the loss of our father, did heal with time. My family prospered and all was well, til deep one winter, a freezing spell. It must have been late in December, yes! Christmas Eve as I remember!

I'd stayed out longer than I meant, lost in the woods the night I spent. Until a few hours before break of dawn, I'd stalked, hunted and tracked a fawn. I'd like to say his escape was narrow, but I had missed with every arrow. When I accepted that he'd got away, I realised it close to break of day.

(As he is speaking the lighting comes up down stage right or left and shows a young man creeping through a woods)

In a part of woods, I hadn't been before, which way was home I wasn't sure. I made my way as best I could but felt something eerie was in the wood. I heard a rustling in a pine, which sent a shiver down my spine! I began to feel I was not alone, something followed, something unknown. I asked myself "Have I stalker or is it just a late night walker" - I knew so late this made no sense and as fear griped me my muscles tensed.

As I travelled ever cautious, my nerves so bad caused feelings nauseous. I felt this presence closing down, but all around me there was no sound. The hairs were standing on my neck, for direction, I could not stop to check. Just when overwhelmed with fear, it passed, and back to thinking clear! I'd been so afraid, things seemed dire, I hadn't felt the need for fire. Now freezing cold but found my way, I made haste for break of day.

(Light comes up down stage centre to reveal a girl sitting there alone, and he slowly makes his way toward her)

After only a short time walking I seen a creature warranting stalking! In a clearing that opened up to me, sat a girl alone on a fallen tree. As I approached she asked "Who's there?" I answered soft so not to scare.

Boy: "Just a hunter from local village, sick of eating crop and tillage"

Rabu: Such anxious thoughts I was laden as I happened upon this comely maiden, her beauty was intoxicating; I had to have her, if just for mating. Her skin was pale but not sickly, her lips red as roses prickly. Her eyes beautiful big and deep, it was like a dream though without sleep? Her beauty made the world seem still, on my approach, I felt a chill.

Boy: Why art thou in the woods at night? Did thou get lost before moonlight?

Girl:　Yes, from my master's home I ran away, now I'm lost and pray for day!

Boy:　And no-one knows that you've gone? Day break is near, it won't be long?

Girl:　No, I wanted to be treated right and that is why I've taken flight.

Boy:　Where will you go? You need a friend, maybe service I can lend?

Girl: You are so kind, but I don't know. Can you take me from this snow? For I am hungry, cold and weak, somewhere warm where we may speak.
Boy: Yes but first there's something you must do for me, for nothing in this world is free!

Girl: What is it from me, you would ask, I hope I'm fitting for your task!

Boy: Oh you are, for you I'm yearning; my body with desire's burning!

Girl: Huh not that! You ask too much, that's why I left my masters clutch! Please leave me, I don't want your aid, I see what sordid plan you've made!

Boy: Just this once and you will see that I will take good care of thee!

Girl: No! Now stop! Leave me I bade, I will not be your chambermaid!

Boy: I don't think you comprehend, your body to me you must lend, please come to me I must insist, I will be gentle, please don't resist.

Rabu: I was in some spellbound trance, and she fell to the ground at my advance. In seconds I was over her, bent on doing acts impure! I grabbed her in a rough embrace; the skin was cold on her hands and face. I stopped, and thought "what's come over me," a change in her then I could see. Her eyes had widened and colour changed, she bore a smile so sly, so strange.

(He gets off her and scuffles backwards, they both rise to their feet, and the girl has an evil grin)
Boy: I'm sorry I don't know how I lost my sense…….
but you seem amused and not so tense. You done this,
you bewitched me, for I am gentle, all can see!

(She walks toward him confidently and speaks accusingly)

Girl: Ha, you weren't so gentle when pinned me down and had me squirming on the ground!

Boy: Who are you and why are you here, I felt your eyes
their sinister leer.

(He realises she's a vampire and tries to pay her homage)

Nothing about you seems the same; huh you've caught
me, for I'm your game! Ah I see you are so very clever
do you use such cunning in each endeavour?

Girl: I could just catch you and begin my feast but I like the sport for I'm no beast!

Boy: Of all the creatures I do admire, none as beautiful as
Madame Vampire.

Girl: Ha although I enjoy your flattery there will be no escape for thee. It would foolish don't you think, for me to waver this chance to drink

Boy: But surely you can catch another, the lord or baron or his brother, for they are big and your wits are keen, but I am small skinny and lean

Girl: And why should I not drink fresh blood? If slaying me possible, you would!

Boy: I would not, I do declare, on my mother's life I swear! Can't you find it in your heart to give a poor boy another start?

Girl: And let a hunter go on living, without a drop of blood being given? Tell me have you family? Or are you all alone like me?

Boy: I live with the miller and no other, though I have my mother, sisters and brother! Although in you I've met a rival, my life is crucial to their survival.

Girl: And what about the girl you curt, or are there any of this sort?

Boy: Little time to this I've lent, between work and hunt, my time is spent!

Girl: The miller, is he, an aged man? Has he grown fat on beer and ham?

Boy: He's not as old as one would think, though he is fond of food and drink!

Girl: What of wife and family? Oppose you to being wed would he?

Boy: I don't think he'd pay much mind; he's always drunk and fully blind!

(*Begging and frustrated*)
Why all these questions, I do not see, please Madame please let me be!

Girl: I am sensitive to your plight, although a creature of the night. I think now better of your deal, away and to your house we'll steal.

Boy: No! For you will kill me or my master, either way it spells disaster!

Girl: Ah don't you want me anymore; I can't lie helpless on your floor!

(*Angrily*)

Boy: That wasn't me it's not me still, violation for me, holds no thrill. That was your own wicked spell; you toyed with me until you fell. No deal with you, I can make, for while you are here my life's at stake.

Girl: Invite me to come to your home, no longer round these woods we'll roam. And I can stay there as your mate, we'll have parties until it's late. And only every now and then, I'll drain one of towns' drunken men. And you will have a prosperous life, with all men envying your perfect wife!

Boy: And you think for me, my life is set? Leading innocent people to their death! With sins like this I could not live, nor could God in Heaven me forgive!

Girl: Then you leave me little choice; I hope your flesh is firm but moist!

Boy: No wait, please yield, I will agree but how can I live safe with thee?

Girl: On pain of death we'll take an oath that neither will the other smote.

Boy: If I slay you my heart be still

Girl: May sun burn me if you I kill

(Lights go down at down stage and come up, up stage on Rabu)

Rabu: So we made a story worthy of telling and I took the Vampire to my dwelling. She allowed the miller live a while, then she took him in true vampire style.

(Lights come up, up stage; she is sitting with her legs across a man)

Let him believe for him her lusting, sat on his lap, grinding, thrusting. When she leaned in to kiss his neck, she bit and drank but gave no peck.

(Lights go down and come back up with a few men and girl on stage)

For years we spent in my home town, she always smiled, I only frowned. All the men thought her my wife, my days and nights both filled with strife. She wore tight corset and short dress, with all the men

she'd flirt and mess. They'd laugh at me and call me 'fool' say 'if she were mine she'd follow rule.' We'd have people round for drink, into a choice of necks her fangs could sink.

(*There are three men on the couch and the girl sitting on one's knee*)

Man 1: For male company she is fond, come here my dear so we may bond.

Man 2: Away with you, home to your wife or you'll find yourself under her knife. It's with me she'll spend the night, and she'll have pleasure till morn and light.

(*He grabs her and pulls her on to his knee, she's smiling and* laughing)

Girl: Gentlemen, what is it that you think of me, for I am married or can't you see.

(*As third man is talking he stands to his feet, takes her hand and stands her up*)

Man 3: Aye, to a fool who's weak and blind, come bed with me I'll treat thee kind.

Girl: Oh and you are all-seeing, tough and strong, with a man like you do I belong?

Man 3: I do not claim to be so great but am man of stature on this estate. I am no simple man of leisure and when with me you're sure of pleasure. I will make you feel such bliss, your entire body I'll caress, I'll kiss. And from this night on for me I'll be keen as I'll take you places you've never been.

Girl: Big words and I believe you would, but what of style of your manhood.

(Everyone laughs, He flies into a rage, orders other two out)

Man 3: You leave, and take him too, a lesson in manner's I'll teach to you!

(The men leave and she steps to him and takes his arms in her hand, or gently rubs his face or puts her hands on his chest)

Girl: I'm sorry, be calm, was just a joke, come here your anger and pain I'll choke. That's it relax your troubled head, and come to couch to sit, or bed?

(He grabs her by the shoulder and pushes her to her knees quite aggressively)

Man 3: On your knees is where you'll start, and taste my manhood my little tart.

Girl: Ah I see now, you're a man that's strong and keen, I'll do things to you, you've never seen. No need for force, no need for haste, men like you I love to taste.

(She puts her hands on his hips and the lights go down, there is a horrific scream)

Act Two

(Lights come up, up stage on Rabu and down stage on an older lying on the couch and the female Vampire)

Rabu: For thirty long years we lived side by side, and she drained me of both strength and pride. There seemed no point in practising faith when helping a Vampire lay her bait. When I was a man of just forty-nine I contracted plague and had little time. Close to death I began to grieve, and she decided that me she'd leave.

Stas: You're leaving! But what of me, Am to die alone? I see!

Girl: I have lingered here for far too long, and you're only good to me if strong. Besides, I know me, you will not miss, you're free now, is this not your wish?

Stas: You've taken everything that once was me, now close to death; and now I'm free? How long here I'll linger, only time will tell, all that waits for me is death, then hell! To spend eternity in hellish torment, when I already a lifetime in this manner spent.

Girl: You enjoyed it when I shared your bed, or is this also sin which pains your heart, your head.

Stas: Still in your words I can't take stock, I'm dying, you're leaving, but still you joke and mock!

Girl: For all the sins that you have committed and all the time we've spent, you could ask your God's forgiveness or can you not repent?

Stas: Heaven will not take me, I will not pass the gate, and all that waits for me I fear is torture, pain and hate.

He is close to tears and pauses for a moment then gets an idea)

Take away my illness and before I get much worse, turn me to a Vampire, be it gift or be it curse!

Girl: You want to be Vampire, I thought you did despise, you too want to draw in prey with a spell of lust and lies. You want to sink your teeth, into the neck and vein, hear that gasp for final breath as you taste their fear, their pain!

Stas: Yes, yes I want all that, though I know that it is wrong, I just can't take this anymore I've been in pain so long! Though hell is what I deserve for choices that I've made, to spend more time in torment, I'm too weak, I'm too afraid.

Girl: I will make you Vampire, creature of the night, but after I have done this, it's then that I'll take flight. For young Vampires, they are unruly, they're like a naughty child, and they want a bite of everyone, so untamed, so wild!

Stas: I should have let you kill me when out there in the wood, because of my cowardice, now I too will hunt for blood. So we've come then to the closure, the end now of

69

our deal…… When you make me Vampire, should I expect to feel?

Girl: You wake first, and strange is how you feel, drawn to feed on anything, something breathing for a meal. You must remember, you're not to make a scene; if you must make a kill, you must also make it clean! For a few villagers you might kill, a few more you could fight, but there are only so many you could take, before impaled or it comes bright. You look as though you're ready, it's time to pierce our veins; soon you'll be strong and healthy, with no more fears or pains!

(*She leans over him and the lights go down; lights come back up on Rabu the narrator*)

Rabu: So she pierced both our wrists and from one another drank, then I drifted into slumber and further and deeper sank. For days and days I did not wake, all I did was sleep, and when I finally rose, I felt compelled, a life to reap!

I looked into a mirror; I was young again, so I waited until nightfall to hunt in the world of men. Out of my dwelling into the street I crept, it's there I saw my sister, but she saw me and wept. She said "I've heard in your house be demon, though I could not believe, but now I see it for myself, you have this night to leave."

Then and there I should have slain her, there were too many in the street, so I lingered in the shadows, till I nabbed some other little treat. That night I drained a life, I sat and drank my fill; then to cave in woods I stole, for good I left the mill. The next night when I woke and I began to rise, the wind carried voices through the trees to my surprise!

Pause because rhythm is changing)

I stepped out to the moonlit night and the woods were a glow with torches light. Hundreds hunting, by the sounds, so many voices so many hounds! It was me they hunted, it was no game, it was clear to me one said my name. So I made a dash, I tried to flee, but they had set a trap for me, I bit and fought and got away, but vowed that I'd return one day.

The next few years I spent prowling, like the hunting wolf, stalking, growling. I picked off people in the night; they'd freeze with shock then die in fright. I moved through countryside and city, picking off the proud and pitied.

Night times spent prowling in the dark and in deep slumber by song of lark. Never really interacting, and always feeling there's something lacking. Till one night resolved to show my face, I went for stroll in a public place. This did change my circumstances as I was met with pleasant glances. Mostly by the female folk, they bowed their head and gently spoke. They were curious to my surprise, I felt them looking, I could feel their eyes. I realised then I shared the spell, of the Vampire into whose trap I fell.

As I walked on I began to smile and took note of how to dress in style. No longer round the streets I roamed, invited to parties, balls and homes.

(*Stas comes on stage in fine clothes, he walks around the stage all the cast walk on and off in pairs and curtsy or bow like at a party*)

There was no more hunting like a beast, on the aristocracy I would feast. Invited to manner and palace halls, for the most lavish and expensive balls.

(*People come on stage in mask walk around, two masked girls pay a lot of attention to Stas, and it's a masquerade ball so there is music, music fades and lights go down*)

Each woman I choose would be my flower, as exercised my fiendish power.   Feeling overpowering love or lust, to have me, they would simply must. And when I got them to my room its then that they would meet their doom.

(*Lights come back up, two dead girls on couch, bloodied necks; Stas is standing in front of a mirror, cleaning his face and fixing his cloths as he speaks he speaks it's to the bodies and then the mirror*)

Stas: I'm sorry ladies, though you were both so fine, I was not content with tonight's wine. I enjoyed your giggles and gentle teasing, but your taste to me is far more pleasing. A messy business, and one must be clean, untidiness, must not be seen. For a gentleman, it is not fitting, like cursing, fighting or even spitting. I'm sure that you would both agree, that being refined, is what is key. And yes, Stas, that's what you are, no longer a beast, you've come so far. Stas?.. It's time to bid this name adieu, what will you call yourself……. Rabu!

Act Three

Rabu: Thirty years since I'd left the mill, in a new town and seeking thrill. An angelic creature I did see, through the street light, coming close to me!

(Lights come up on a dimly lit stage, a street setting, a girl walks into the light and stops to tie her laces, Rabu2's voice is heard but you cannot see from where)

Rabu2: What have we here? A tasty bite, out here all helpless in the night!

Clara: Who is it? Who is that speaking, and from the darkness at me peaking?

Rabu2: Just a man from a land near here, I seek lodgings and ale or beer.

Clara: I can point you toward our local inn, its cosy and there's ale and gin.

Rabu2: Company with me won't you keep, for to drink alone would make one weep.

Clara: I'm sorry sir, my curfew I cannot break, and of ale and gin I don't partake.

Rabu2: Well maybe just walk me to the door, and we can talk a little more.

Clara: I really can't for I'm already late, perhaps a chat at a later date!

(*One line from Rabu the narrator*)

Rabu: I thought I'd jump her to prevail as my spell on her did seem to fail.

Rabu2:   My restrain is being sorely tested as sinister interests in you, I've vested.

(*A man steps into the light, speaks to the girl and then to Rabu2 who is still in the shadows*)

Brother: Clara what is it, that has you keeping? Who is that from the darkness peeping?

Clara: I don't know father but he is scary, he's coming closer please be weary.

Brother: You dare keep my daughter late; announce yourself, your name now state.

(*Rabu2 steps out into the light*)

Rabu2:   I'm sorry Sir did I offend, a moment and your ear please lend.

Clara: No father! For he might seem charming but he is menacing, it's quite alarming.

Brother: Huh brother, is it really you I'm seeing or are my senses all but fleeing.

Rabu2: Yes, yes it's me, it's been sometime! Is this young angel of your line?

Clara: You mean to say you know this man, he is blood, and of our clan?

Brother: This is your uncle, been long away, my heart rejoices to see this day.

Rabu2: To see you now my heart does sore, and your offspring! Are there more?

Clara: Father, this man I have no trust in.

Brother: We do not talk that way of kin! Come brother to my household, we'll have the stories of your travels told. We'll stay up late and drink and eat, and my....your family you will meet.

Rabu2:   For this for years I have been praying, come young lady, I was merely playing.

Brother: Come at once and stop your nonsense. Don't make a happy moment tense.

Rabu2:   Maybe another time would suit, she's just nervous, I think it cute.

Brother: No brother must be this night, and you will see Becca's delight.

Rabu2:   Rebecca lives? And lives with you? My visit with her is long overdue. What of Sara where is she? Does she also live with thee?

Brother: No Sara passed a year ago, the consumption, her death was slow. But enough of this, we must make haste or we'll miss super without a taste.

(*Lights fade come a minute later in a house setting, there is a middle aged woman, and a young couple and a boy in the room, Rabu's brother and Clara enter from side of stage*)

Brother: Come in come in its desperate cold and for weather like this I fear we're too old.

(*Rabu2 steps in from the side of the stage as his brother announces him*)

Brother: Your Uncle is here, we must celebrate, Sofia! Set an extra plate

(*When his brother turns and faces him he is shocked*)

Brother: Stas! Your face! Where is your age? You look too young for your life's stage! You are my senior of fourteen years, but look weathered only as Imelda's peers.

(*Rebecca comes on stage and descends the stairs as she speaks*)

Rebecca: Demons do not age as we do, thankfully their kind are few. Why did you invite him in, he'll show no mercy even with kin.

Brother: Rebecca what is this, has your brain gone weak, this is our brother of whom you speak!

Rebecca: Our brother died a long time ago, he is a demon, this I know.

Rabu2: Rebecca, let your heart not fret, it's been thirty years since we have met! I did not come to do thee harm, here is no cause for your alarm. I was curious I must confess, to see my family but not cause stress!

Rebecca: You should not have let him in; he's an abomination of dark and sin. There's nothing he says that you can trust, he lives for blood, and women's lust. I spent years working to get us away, *(To Rabu)* **but always for your soul I'd pray. Why have you come? Why are you here? To kill us all or just spread fear?**

Brother: Please explain so my heart be lightened, but in private for the child is frightened.

Rebecca: Not in private for it spells danger, he is not our brother, he's a dark, dark stranger. Made immortal by unholy deal, he now harvests lives for blood's his meal. I never told you for your protection, I see this was flawed now on reflection.

Brother: Please say she's wrong brother; this can't be true, for I have such fond memories of you!

Rabu2: Brother I'm afraid that it is no mistake, but your lives I have not come to take. Although Rebecca drove me away, they ambushed me and tried to slay. Some of their lives I managed to take, I avoided death by wooden stake. But all this I think I can forgive as in harmony I think that we can live.

Rebecca: You forgive me then of my crime, has your wrath weakened with passing time.

Rabu2: Hmm, of forgiveness I am surely able, would you forgive Becca if turned tables?

Rebecca: I'm sorry, how can I make amends, for a life in fear and regret I've spent.

Rabu2: Would you accept me again and hold me dear, and call me brother and erase your fear.

Rebecca: Of course, oh brother, you I did miss, for so long this is your sister's wish.

(Rebecca trying to hide her fear embraces Rabu with a hug)

Rabu2: It feels good to hold you in my arms, but I am weary of my sisters' charms. With hurt before, my heart was broken; now for loyalty will thou grant me token.

Rebecca: What is it brother that you need, not a life, I beg, I plead.

Rabu2: I want our family to reunite, you are all blind, I offer sight.

Brother: I fear I do not understand, for we see well as any man.

Rabu2:   Join my ranks, become vampire and over all these lands we'll sire. As a coven we can rain supreme, it's of our own kingdom that I dream.

Brother: Leave my house, enough of this, and don't return, that is my wish.

Rabu2:   I don't think you understand, I offer immortality, at my right hand.

Brother: It's you who does not understand, or did you not hear my last demand.

Rabu2:   And who are you to make demands; you have no power, no servants, and no lands. If you join me you'll have all this so don't be so hasty to dismiss. Seven in this meagre home, why not a castle with grounds to roam. We'll have servants, be men of leisure; we'll only rise for blood or pleasure. You need not worry if children fed and if their warm while in their bed. No more sickness and loved ones dying, no more feeling pain or crying.

Brother: You are a sin against creation, of what you talk would bring damnation. Now leave! I insist you must and take your talk of sin and lust.

Rabu2:   Ah I see, well before I leave, there's something owed here I do believe. As a young man I looked after you, surely you think something is due.

Brother: We never asked you for your aid, nothing is owed, no deal was made.

Rabu2: You and Rebecca have both grown old; I kept hunger from you and the cold. It's thanks to me you're at this age; your ungratefulness fills me with rage.

Brother: Well what is it you feel your owed if ours to give, on you bestowed.

Rebecca: No, no, nothing he says is worthy of trust, slay him now, let him turn to dust.

Brother: No! To our home, him I lead, so he will leave here with no blood shed.

Rabu2: Ha, Rebecca, I knew you were not genuine, only your looks have changed with time!
(To his brother) Thanks to me you've offspring and wife, what is owed? Life for life!

Brother: What?

Rabu2: We were young and you in need, and for you and our sisters I'd hunt to feed. I stalked my prey in dark and late and one Christmas Eve I met my fate. It was then she began to steal my life, the woman you knew as my wife. I lived a life both hard and long, but finally before she was gone, I was sick and things looked dire, so I asked for gift to be made Vampire. Then by my own sisters I was betrayed, for this the debt must be repaid.

Rebecca: I knew it, you'll get no life to take away, and you'll still be here come break of day.

Rabu2: I won't! For if you do not offer a life, I'll take you, brother, offspring and wife!

Rebecca: **The answer I fear I already know, but Stas, won't you please just go?**

Rabu2: Although I enjoyed your begging tone, I won't be leaving here alone.

Brother: **Then I offer myself as what you feel you're due,** *(there is a pause then he hugs everyone and mutters goodbyes then walks across the stage ahead of Rabu, everyone is weeping)* **be safe, for I love each and all of you.**

(As Rabu turns to walk out Rebecca runs at him with a wooden stake shouting)

Rebecca: **STAS!**

(He turns and catches the stake and turns it on her)

Rabu2: Now look what you have made me do, ha I never thought I'd run you through *(laughs)*

Brother: **Rebecca!**

Rabu2: As a youth I fed thee, fitting now that thou feed me.

(Rabu twists the stake in her and she whimpers and he goes to bit her neck...Everyone is crying and scared, and then brother runs for Rabu)

Brother: **Stas you monster!**

(Rabu subdues him looks straight in his face and speaks then bites his neck and drops him to the floor)

Rabu2: I am not Stas I am Rabu! Stas is dead, now so are you!

(Lights go down and come up on Rabu the narrator)

Rabu: Then I killed all except my nephews' wife; they each fought hard to keep their life.

(Lights come up and bodies everywhere except Imelda (his nephews wife) who looks terrified and the vampire)

Rabu2: Come now, all debts are paid, come to me don't be afraid.

(He walks towards her she is frozen with fear, he puts his spell on her as he stands her up, and he whispers in her ears, and then kisses her neck)

Rabu2: Though nothing left is owed or due, your virtue I will take from you.

(He leans her back and lowers her to the ground, kissing her neck and beginning to undress her, lights go down and come up on Rabu the narrator)

Rabu: Then I did take my nephews wife, I took her virtue, then took her life. I hope it's plain now for you to see that there is no way out for thee!

Marie: And what of the child, did you toy, you didn't really kill the boy?

Rabu: Of course I did, for I don't feel, only lust and want of meal.

Marie: The Almighty's wrath will fall on you and you'll receive all you are due.

Rabu: Your God for me holds no threat, even his servants I have put to death.

Marie: You mean you say you've killed a priest and on blessed blood you have had feast.

Rabu: A priest is merely a man in cloth, a mere human who can be sold or bought. Not only did I take one's life I also took a bride of Christ. In a small town of Catholic faith I seen a beauty with whom I'd mate. Bored with merely drinking blood some sport I welcomed and she looked good. I'd test my power and have some fun as I turned my attentions to this young nun.

(Lights to come up on stage in parts where story is being told and show bits of conversation or action; dialogue in the present tense)

Rabu: It was a challenge I must admit, in her life of prayer, I did not fit. My attention and strong persistence at first was met with strong resistance. But I could see she was wearing down, as a women lay beneath that gown. My attention had not gone unseen, by the priest, whose eyes and wits were keen. He approached me and asked "why interested" said "I will not see that girl molested.'

I said "with her I merely like to talk as we take a harmless moonlit walk." So our keeping company he forbade, but stronger our connection made. As forbidden love will bring desire and the thoughts of me she did admire. For a time we could not speak so much but by letter we would keep in touch. From her writing it was clear to see she battled with feelings for me. Till one night she could take no more, and like you, knocked upon my door. But with her I did not stop my spell and being near me more in love she fell.

As I told her such love could be no sin to remove her habit I did begin. Just when her virtue I had taken, came a banging sound like my door was breaking.

(*Lights come up down stage Rabu2 is dressing himself. The woman is there with blankets around her / undergarments on. In comes the priest, sees the nun and flies into a rage*)

Priest: What's this? What's this? What have you done? You defiled this girl, defiled this nun! And you! How could you disregard your vow? You must dress and leave this house right now!

(*The girl stands to leave and Rabu2 pushes her back down*)

Rabu2: How dare you just come barging in, to invade one's home is that not sin?

Priest: Sin! Oh brazen are the words now spoken, when an oath with God wickedly broken. You sir for thine part in this will suffer death and heaven miss. As both of you,

you have forsaken when a bride of Christ's virtue you've taken.

Rabu2: And tell me father, how am I to suffer death, should I fear with you my fate be met? Should my heart now be filled with strife as a man of cloth threatens my life?

Priest: You think this time to joke and mock, well in my words you should take stock. I will tell the people of your wicked deed as with a nun you spread your seed. And they will do on to you what is just, as be punished for vile sin you must!

Rabu2: Then maybe I will not permit you leave, and for your own life here you will grieve.

Priest: You talk in riddles, is that a threat, you dare not threaten my life with death.

Rabu2: Call it promise or call it threat but here with me your fate be met. You made mistake is it now clear, no one of cloth is leaving here!

(As the priest is saying these next four lines Rabu2 stands the girl up with her back to the priest and kisses her neck but he doesn't stop staring at the priest as he does so, before the last line she falls to the floor dead)

Priest: I knew you bad, seen just at night, never seen in day or light. Evil in you does run deep, but from you slowly begins to seep. I feel your eyes, their gaze is strong......to this world you don't belong. Lucifer it cannot be, for you look so human all can see!

Rabu2: *(laughs)* **Satan no, he I'm not, though through his power I am begot. My body born to the world of man but new life for me has since began. On mortals, feeding, years I've spent, on violation my mind is bent.**

(Priest backs off shaking with fear, Rabu2 powerfully, slowly and confidently advances on him)

Priest: An Angel cometh to fight thy beast; on no more blood will thou feast! And you'll finally meet thy maker, no more evil from life blood taker!

Rabu2: No Angel comes to save thee, Priest, and if one did on them I'd feast!

(Priest begins to pray the Our Father, Rabu2 reaches him and holds him by the throat)

Waste your last breath and pray, you've seen your last night and day. I feed on this, feed on your fear, you waste your breath there's no God here!

(Lights go down, and come back up on Rabu and Marie)

Rabu: Compassion I do not possess, it's near to dawn, on we must press. So tell me, on you am I to feast? Or will you join me, and be a beast?

Marie: To live like you and kill my own, I think I'd rather die here, alone! I know now, for me it is too late, I know what's coming, I accept my fate!

But before you kill me and end all this, make me feel your love, and bliss! Not leave this world with no loved one near, with no comfort and consumed by fear!

Rabu: Of course, I will grant your final wish and enchant you before the fatal kiss. For it feels good when one is willing, even when their life blood spilling!

(Romantic music plays, violin preferably, this all happens very slow and lines are delivered very slowly and one at a time, she backs off down rostrum slowly teary eyed and afraid, he follows her looking menacing but as he nears centre stage his demeanour is changing, becoming slowly soft and hers is becoming less frightened and sad)

Look deep and feel loving eyes; forget your fears and the world of lies! Come to me let us embrace, for in my dreams I see your face. Come to me I'll treat thee kind, soft gentle love is on my mind. Come my dear; come take my hand, listen to what your heart demands.

(She walks toward him in a trance like state; some gentle music can be heard, she is almost smiling)

Marie: Feelings fade of fear or dread, music and beauty now fill my head.

(He takes her by the hand and leads her down the stairs, and says the next lines very passionately)

Rabu: The music heard is in our hearts, for souls in love who'll never part. It's created in them, deep inside when fate has made their paths collide.

(He puts a hand to her face and she melts into it and drops gently to her knees while he still cups her face, he looks into her eyes as he speaks, and as he's speaking he brings her in closer, and tilts her head back, exposing her neck, between each line he kisses it)

Marie: Oh Rabu, I feel your love, take me please I've given up. Freely offered I am to you, take your time and do with me what you would do.

Rabu: You look so beautiful, so elegant but time for us is all but spent.

Maria: No, don't send me love from your side; I cannot live with peace denied.

Rabu: Of course not, it's here with me you'll find your peace and with my kiss your soul's release. Your gentle touch so soft and shy, its time my dear you're peace is nigh!

(He leans her right back on close of last line and bits in, her eyes widen sharply, she moans and stiffens and as she goes limp and her eyes close the lights and curtains come down)

The End

By Dermot Nelson, 2011

When Santa Turned Bad

Narrator: *Our story begins, and so it is told, far,*
far away in the snow covered North
Pole:

There once was a Christmas were
Santa turned bad; he made wee girls
and wee boys unhappy and sad.

But before Christmas was ruined for
ever you see, a miracle happened by a
Christmas tree.

If you can imagine the North Pole
where it's cold, there the story begins
and here's how it's told...

SCENE 1

Scene begins with Mrs Clause and some elves on stage.
Mrs Clause is walking around a kitchen
setting giving out about Santa not being
prepared and how it's the same every
year.

Mrs Clause: Oh that Santa at Christmas, oh for God
sake, I spent the whole morning baking
and he ate every cake.

And as for last year, well Rudolf was lame, Santa tried to use torches but it wasn't the same.

He crashed into a house, a tree top and wall, it's a wonder the kids got their presents at all.

Elf: And the year before that he'd gotten so stout, he went down a chimney but couldn't get out

Elves all laugh

Mrs Clause: Oh! It's no laughing matter but we were in luck, 25 firemen helped get him unstuck.

Enter Santa in a panic; his hat is tucked into his trousers

Santa: My hat, my hat I can't find my hat, oh now where's my list, oh no what's happened to that!

Elves laugh, Mrs Clause walks over and pulls the hat out and hands it to Santa

Mrs Clause: Oh for God sake, will you stop being so silly, keep your hat on your head for outside (even inside) it's chilly!

Santa: Ho, ho, ho, oh silly me, Why thank you my dear, but the naughty / nice list, I've lost it I fear.

Mrs Clause: Have you checked in your coat or under
                the bed? If it wasn't screwed on, why
                you'd lose your head!

Santa: What is it my dear, you seem awfully
                cross?

Mrs Clause: Well 'I' do the work and they call YOU
                the boss! *(She says they while pointing
                at elves)*

Santa puts his arm over her shoulder

Santa: Awh You know you're important, sure
                we all think your great, If it wasn't for
                you we'd be in some state!

Elves all nod in agreement

Mrs Clause: What's gotten into you? Have you had
                some beer?

She pushes his arm off, Santa winks at audience

Santa: Eh....Why, why, why not at all Honey,
                it's just Christmas cheer

Knocking on the door sound

Mrs Clause: Huh it must be my Mummy, I'm
                expecting no other

Mrs Clause is smiling, Santa looks terrified

Santa: That's my cue to leave, I must, eh, eh, I
                must visit my brother!

Santa hurries off stage and Mrs Clause is left shaking her head.

(End of Scene One)

SCENE 2

Narrator: **Now old Mother Nature was Santa's mother in law, but each time she seen Santa she'd point out a flaw.**

Like he was too fat, or his Elves too skinny or too much long hair on his chinny chin chinny.

She never wanted Mrs Clause marrying Santa you know, for she liked Jack Frost, he worked with the snow.

Mother Nature: Hello my dear, oh, don't you look a mess, it's probably with Christmases holiday stress.

Mrs Clause: Oh stop it mummy, sure I'm all over the place, there's so much to be done and I'm blue in the face.

Mother Nature: I'll put on some tea, now sit down there you, and while I'm here I'll see what's to do.

Mrs Clause: You could start with the weather; did you make that big storm? Could we not have one winter here were its nice and warm.

Mother Nature: Now stop that moaning, worse weather we've felt, and if I made it warm here the North Pole would melt!

So where is your husband?

Where is himself, the big ball of jolly, that overgrown Elf!

Elves: HEY!!

Mrs Clause: Away to his brothers or so he said, there's so much to do and he's not long out of bed.

Mother Nature: Has he got a brother? I thought he had none!

Mrs Clause: Well since he heard you were coming, all of a sudden he's one!

Mother Nature: Tut tut tut, typical, could you not have married someone like Jack Frost, he's never down chimneys and never gets lost.

Mrs Clause: Jack Frost isn't nice, he's even cold in his heart, now I love my Santa so mummy don't start.

    I know he's a clutz that's sometimes in trouble, but he makes me smile, so don't burst my bubble!

    He's kind and he's fun and he makes me giggle, and I love when he laughs and his belly does jiggle.

Mother Nature makes a getting sick gesture

Mother Nature: Okay, okay, I'll give him a chance but he's always so jolly, and those jumbo red pants!

    (End of Scene Two)

SCENE 3

Narrator: *So old Mother Nature agreed that she would be nice, and she eased off the storm but they soon paid the price.*

    Through the snow crept a Nymph, naughty and niggling, I've found Santa's workshop to himself Twist was giggling.

Twist (Nymph): Oh Santa's workshop, now's my chance to be bad, I'll make all those Elves cry and be sad!

Ho, ho, ho is heard off stage, and Twist hides then Santa and some Elves enter

Santa: AIMEE? AIMEE? Now where's Aimee Elf, the littlest one?

Elves shrug

Elf 2: She's not spoken a word since her life has begun.

Elf: Oh who knows Santa, she's always off on her own, (*To crowd*) she can't speak or laugh not even a tone.

Elves all shake their heads and say Awh (*elf(s) will hold up a sign saying awh*)

Santa: Oh if Aimee where here, she'd find my list; she once found my lost reindeers through thick snow and thick mist!

Santa's three daughters enter and hug Santa

Heidi: Hiye Father Christmas!

Hilda: We came to say hey

Harmony: What have you lost this time? Are you feeling okay?

Santa:	Ho, ho, ho hello my girls! Oh there's so much to do, it's almost Christmas Eve and presents are due.
	My naughty nice list I can't seem to find, oh who's naughty, who's nice it's boggling my mind.
	The reindeers need feeding, these presents need wrapped, I must find my list and the sleigh isn't packed.
Heidi:	We'll help you Daddy, there's no need to worry, and we'll have these present wrapped up in a hurry.
Hilda:	And the Elves can feed reindeers and pack up your sleigh, and you'll find your list by Christmas Eve day.
Harmony:	Ye, so don't worry Daddy, don't panic or stress and we'll all pull together and sort out this mess.
Santa:	Ho, ho, ho thank you girls, I probably I don't tell you as much as I should, but you are so special and ever so good.

Santa and Elves head off stage as the last elf is going off stage Twist the Nymph grabs the last Elf's hat without being noticed, girls start wrapping presents

Narrator:	*So Santa went off on his list finding quest and the elves packed the sleigh with toys destined for chests.*
	And as for the Nymph, a plan formed in his mind, sneaky and cruel, mean and unkind.
	He came out from his hide-out disguised as an Elf, he thought....
Twist:	(*to crowd*) I'll use these girls rather then get caught myself.
	Hello girls, helping I see, it will go faster if you include me.
Heidi:	Oh hello I'm Heidi, are you a new Elf.
Hilda:	And hi I'm Hilda, I don't know you myself.
Twist:	Oh, no I'm not new I've been here some time, though I eh, eh, worked with the toys on the assembly line.
Harmony:	Well I am Harmony, what is your name; I bet it's real cute; all you Elves are the same.

Harmony pulls his cheek and he pushes her hand away

Twist:	My name is Twi....ch, on, on, on account of my nose, it's like Pinocchio except my nose doesn't grow.

Heidi:	Does that mean your nose would twitch if you lie.
Twist:	Yes but since being a young Elf I don't even try.
Narrator:	Then Twist began to poison their minds, saying things about Santa of a terrible kind.
Twist:	Why is that Santa loves other kids more, you probably don't think so but are you quite sure.
	He spends the whole year making more than one toy, oh so many presents for each girl and each boy.
	On Christmas Eve why isn't he here, he's all over the world having pudding and beer.
	If he was my dad I'd want him to know, that love for his own kids he should probably show.
Narrator:	*They fell into his trap and under his spell, as he twisted the truth and such lies he did tell.*
Heidi:	Well how will we show him that we are here, not just to wrap presents and spread Christmas Cheer?

Hilda: I have a good mind to tell him myself,
                that I am his daughter and not just the
                help.

Twist: Hmm well what of a potion, what
                would you think; you'd see a new Santa
                with one little drink.

Harmony: Oh can you get us a potion and then he
                will see and he'll spend his Christmas
                with us by the tree.

(End of Scene Three)

SCENE 4

Narrator: *So Twist gave them the potion and*
                again he did hide and he laughed
                through the night, for he was rotten
                inside.

                And the girls poured the potion into
                Santa's tea; it would be the next
                morning before the change they would
                see.

**When Santa woke up on Christmas
Eve morn, he was not the same Santa,
but full of venom and scorn.**

**He got up quite early and mounted his
sleigh and left the North Pole while in
bed the Elves lay.**

**Little Aimee Elf always first out of bed
found something funny, Twists hat
from his head.**

*Aimee Elf comes on stage and yawns and picks up twists
hat and then Santa's list.*

**Not only that but she found Santa list,
she looked to find Santa but thought
him she had missed.**

*She goes on and off stage on both sides and comes on
and shrugs her shoulders and holds up
the list.*

**But how would he know who was
naughty and nice, he'd never have
gone without checking it twice.**

*Evil laughing is heard and Aimee hides as Twist comes
on stage.*

**Then she heard laughing not of the
North Pole, it was cunning and
naughty so to hiding she stole.**

Twist:	A bad Santa I've made, oh isn't it great, rude and obnoxious, ha what's Christmas' fate?
	And only an Elf's words with the chime of MY bell, saying 'come back Father Christmas' can break my dark spell
	And I lost my bell on my way here, lost in thick snow, NO MORE CHRISTMAS CHEER (*evil laugh*)

Twist goes off stage and Aimee runs about panicking, then she leaves the stage, Mrs Clause and an Elf come on stage

Mrs Clause:	SANTA, OH SANTA, oh where could he be? It's the first time he's been up before me.
Elf:	Maybe he's checking who's naughty and nice, found his old list and is checking twice.

More Elves come on with messages

Elf2:	MRS CLAUSE! THE SLEIGH! THE SLEIGH, it is gone, and the presents where left, oh something is wrong.
Elf3:	LOOK, it's his red magic sack and a note signed by Santa saying 'I'm not coming back.'

Mrs: Oh no he has left, is it cause of me, is it cause I asked him to put up the tree?

(End of Scene Four)

SCENE 5

(Possibly for the narration at the start of this scene have a bad Santa on stage doing the bad acts)

Narrator: ***For the whole day Mrs Clause was unhappy and sad, till it got to the night and they heard Santa had turned bad.***

As reports came in from a far and a wide, Santa had turned nasty, he was different inside.

When in people's houses he ate all their food, if any got up he was pushy and rude.

He picked at his nose and wiped on a chair; he opened up presents that were already there.

He made loads of noise and woke a whole house, he kicked at a dog and stamped on a mouse.

He stole a young boys stuffed teddy bear; he woke a young girl by pulling her hair.

Mrs Clause: Oh my poor Santa what's got into you?
                He's just not himself, oh what will I do?

A knock is heard and Mother Nature comes on stage

Mother Nature: Well hello my dear, did you see the
                news, it seems Santa has stolen a keg
                full of booze.

                You see my dear; can you see your
                folly? I knew that no-one was really
                that jolly (*makes the drinky drinky motion*)

Mrs Clause: No mother it's not Santa, or he's under
                some spell, I know it's not him, I'm his
                wife I can tell.

Mother Nature: Oh, it's the real Santa, he just hid it
                well, listen to me child for your
                mummy can tell.

Mrs Clause gets very upset

Mrs Clause: Stop it now mummy! Oh what will I do,
                I know that's not Santa, I know it's not
                true!

Someone must have found us, though
we're on no map, someone has taken
him, he must be kidnapped!

Mother Nature: Oh I'm sorry child, please do not fret,
we'll figure this out now don't be upset.

Narrator: So while the ladies and Elves tried to
figure it out, little Aimee had gone
searching, in the snow she'd gone out.

She searched for some hours till she
finally found, a bell half snow covered
that lay on the ground.

Then she walked for some hours
without a break or a stop, through
blizzard and cold to Santa's workshop.

*Aimee comes on stage and tries to get everyone's
attention but no one is looking*

Mrs Clause: Yes I see Aimee that's a nice bell but
we're having a crisis or can you not tell.

Elf2: Yes, Aimee why don't you go and wish
by the tree, for bad Santa to let good
Santa go free.

*Narrator: So a frustrated Aimee knelt down by
the tree she wished hard for a voice to
set Santa free.*

Then trying real hard she opened her mouth she moved her tongue and her teeth but no sound came out.

Downhearted and sad she started to weep and out from her mouth there came a wee peep.

She looked all around and thought was that me? Then she spoke her first word by the Christmas tree.

Aimee: Me?

Narrator: *Then she jumped to her feet and ran all about, she got all excited and*

Aimee: I CAN SPEAK!

Narrator: *She did shout*

Aimee: I can talk! I can talk! I even said me; because I made a wish by the Christmas tree!

Narrator: *Then quickly remembering why she made the wish, she ran to save Santa and ran to stop Twist.*

Aimee comes back on main stage area with the bell and rings it so everyone looks at her

Mrs Clause: OH Aimee Elf will you stop with that bell.

Aimee: But I've something to say or can YOU not tell!

Everyone on stage gasps and freezes staring at Aimee and she rings bell saying…….

Aimee: I know what to do, so please me don't dismiss, with a chime from this bell 'Come back Father Christmas!

There is like a magic kind of sound affect, then the sound of a sleigh. Then Santa comes back on stage very confused and clumsy

Santa: Oh what has been happening, I've had such a bad dream, such naughty antics I just want to scream.

Aimee: Oh Santa you're back, then I broke the spell, with a wish by the tree and this magic bell.

Everyone on stage is saying wow

Santa: HUH you can talk Aimee Elf!

Aimee nods her head smiling and Santa walks over and shakes Aimee's hand

Santa: Well thank you so much, but from who came the spell? From whose magic touch and whose magic bell?

Twist and Santa's girls come on stage and Aimee Elf points at them.

Aimee: It's that Elf right there, why he's mean
                    don't you see he tricked your poor girls
                    and they messed with your tea.

Girls have their heads down ashamed Twist goes to
                    leave but Elves stop him

Santa: That's not an Elf it's a Nymph who's
                    named Twist kept away from our home
                    by thick snow and thick mist.

                    What has you here; to be bad is it
                    Twist? You've never been on the nice
                    side of my list!

Twist looks very angry and defiant and clenches his
                    teeth and takes lots of deep breaths in
                    like he's going to shout a lot but
                    suddenly just starts to cry
                    uncontrollably

Twist: Everyone gets presents but with Twist
                    you don't share, since I was a small
                    Nymph nobody's cared.

                    I know I've been naughty and cruel or
                    mean but I've only acted the way I have
                    seen.

                    For no one likes Twist and no friends or
                    romance but I could be good if given
                    the chance.

I've spent so long angry, sad and alone, I just want to find somewhere that I can call home.

All the Elves say Awh (one holds up the awh card to audience)

Santa: Oh poor Twist is that why you act bad? why I had no clue that you were unhappy and sad.

Mrs Clause: Can you use your spells and work through the night, use your magic for good and help put Christmas right?

Santa puts his arm around Mrs Clause; Twist has his head down all sad like a child who's crying.

Santa: And we and the Elves will give you a home and no longer around all alone would you need roam

Santa's Girls: And we'll be your sisters

Elves: And we'll be your friends

BOTH: And over time your sad heart we can mend.

Twist puts his head up nervously and they welcome him to their group with little pats on the back and hand shakes

Narrator:	*So Twist agreed and he helped make Christmas right, He worked with Santa and Elves all through the night.*

And even Mother Nature did lend a hand as she calmed down the weather all over each land.

And Mrs Clause and Santa did give Twist a home and Mother Nature agreed she'd leave Santa alone.

And Santa's three girls realised their folly and their time spent with Santa was then always jolly.

And Twist began to feel such warmth in his heart and to show love and kindness he quickly did start.

And little Aimee Elf whose big voice saved the day is cheered every Christmas with a…

ALL CAST: Hip hip hurray

The End

BY DERMOT NELSON, 2012

POETRY

The Naughty Puppy

There was wee a pup who was awfully bold
His Mummy got cross and him she did scold
But HE didn't like to be told what to do
He just barked and gave cheek, a rapscallion, its
true
He'd bark at the post man, and rip up the mail
He'd dig up the garden and chase his own tail
He'd go out on the road and run after a car
When out for a walk he'd run off real far
His Mummy got crosser and loud she did shout
'Hmp' thought the puppy, 'Mum I'll do without'
So he sneaked out at night, and a way he did run
'I'll live on my own and have lots of fun'
He wandered the streets, he went far and wide
But as he was walking he was changing inside
He got cold and got scared, and soon seen the cost
For now he was hungry, and now he was lost
He heard noise in the night and couldn't find
home
Lonely and scared, round dark streets he roamed
Back home his wee Mummy crept into his room
And over his bed did quietly loom
Always as he slept, she'd kiss him goodnight
When she saw him not there, she took awful fright
She called out his name, looked under his bed
She looked in the cupboard, she scratched at her
head
She asked in the neighbours, she looked in the
town

She called the police, she looked all around
She let out a whimper, a worrying sigh
'Oh where is my puppy' in pain she did cry
'Oh my poor baby you're not really bad
Please just come home' his poor Mummy was sad
'Why did I bark at you, oh why did I scold
I just want you back; it's so dark out and cold'
His Mummy kept looking, without any light
She wouldn't give up, even all through the night
For she loved her wee puppy, when good or when
bad
And the thought of him lost made her hurt, made
her sad
When close to the morning, she heard a
whimpering sigh
She found her wee puppy, and with joy she did cry
She wrapped him all up with a hug and a kiss
She said 'my poor baby, oh you I did miss'
And he felt so safe and warm in her arms
And she was so thankful he'd come to no harm
She said 'never again will I get so mad'
And he said 'no Mummy, I'll no longer be bad'
'Well I'll try not to bark and frighten my pup'
'And I'll try to play nice and not get you wound
up'
I'm so sorry Mummy for making you cry
I'll no longer be bold I won't fib or won't lie'
'And I'm sorry son for shouting as such
I am your Mummy and I LOVE YOU SO MUCH'.
By Dermot Nelson, 2011

The Parrot Who Lost His Voice

There once was a parrot that had lost his voice

He'd have asked you for help if given the choice

He looked up and down, he looked high and low

He looked here and there, he looked to and fro

He tried to ask girls, he tried to ask boys

But when he opened his beak he could barely make noise

So he pecked at a girl, he pecked at a boy

He pecked at a Mummy, he pecked at a toy

He got all excited and flapped all about

He got so upset he wanted to shout

He put his head in the air and tried a BE-GAUWK

But when he opened his beak, all that came was a squawk

Then feeling downhearted, he let out a sigh

Sat on his hunkers, and started to cry

Then a Granny approached and told him 'not to feel bad'

Said 'it's just a sore throat and no need to be sad'

'If you go to the vet, he'll fix it right up'

'Then Parrot once more, you will 'chirp' so cheer up'.

By Dermot Nelson, 2011

Cheese before Bed

Lost in a world of deep, deep slumber, so many
dreams with awe and wonder

The bold young hero doing his duty, fine young
maidens blessed with beauty

It's clear to him, that for him they're lusting, from
frail tight garments their bosoms busting

The only problem he is now laden, which one first,
which fine young maiden

The world is gleaming, the sun is strong, and all of
nature alive with song

Such harmony, such perfect bliss, euphoria must
be close to this

As Heaven unfolds in perfect dreams, it's shattered
by horrific screams

He begins to think, 'Have I been hasty?' as what
unfolds is less than tasty

The hero charged with being a scout, and so he
must, or him they'll doubt

On route to screams, the light, it fades, farewell to
beauty, and peace, he bades

While darkness round him is slowly creeping,
more screams, loud wailing and bitter weeping

The once warm air has now turned cold, the once
brave knight, now not so bold

His dream has taken nasty twist and all around
him there forms a mist

He can't see now, but on he's creeping, the ground
has changed, it's soft and seeping

Behind him now, he hears pain in screech, not his
maidens! He must run to reach

But he cannot see and falls to ground, there's a
person! Though they make no sound

He tries to talk, and then to shake, then realizes,
this was mistake
An arm! It's severed! Now in his hand! And he
now sees what he thought was land
Is Bodies lying mutilated! Woman! Men! Both
violated!
Bodies, severed limbs and heads, eyes still open,
still don't look dead!
Mountains of corpses, so many, so steep, noxious
odours from wretched heaps!
From dark corners sees creatures leering, from
their dens at him their peering
He tries to climb but just keeps stumbling,
desperately praying, climbing, mumbling
He looks, they're coming ever nearer, in moonlight
now he sees them clearer
Monstrous creatures all fangs and drooling, evil
swords men bent on duelling
As they draw near, heart palpitation, he foresees
his death, decapitation!
Body ripped, limb from limb, the end is near and it
looks grim
He can't climb out, he can't escape, they're closing
down, they're at his cape
Just when his faith is all but met, he wakes in his
bed, wakes in a sweat!
Phew just a dream, but felt so real, though back to
first part I could steal
Heart does beat with dreams like these; I hope that
we're not out of cheese!!

By Dermot Nelson, 2010

FALSE

Twisted minds and venomous tongues squirt vile
hatreds in my ear

They're not my friends as I supposed but a nest of
rats I fear

As one turns their head on wretched neck I see
their other face

So convincing and sincere, I break, and they trap
me in this place

Defences down, once more I think, this really is my
friend

But I see the truth as time unfolds it's a sick game
of pretend

To use a hug, a loving gesture, and speak words so
kind

A trait in which a rat would use, a more sick game
you shall not find

By Dermot Nelson, 2011

A TORMENTED HUSBAND

A sickening anger burns in me, I can't tell if it's just

It's confusing! Do I want to know? But it's obvious
that I must

The thoughts of it I cannot bear, Could she be so
vile?

She still meets me with a loving face, a familiar
loving smile

She tells me I seem distant, and asks me for the
why

I know I cannot answer true, I cannot take her lie

She seems so full of venom now, I feel so cruelly
torn

And by the mire in which she spins her lies, my
patience is getting worn

Frustration in me is building, I really must be sure

But if with her I false accuse, will there be a cure

In desperation, I plead with God "let it be mistake"

All ready all my pride has gone, my heart! Inside I
ache

I want to know for certain, I want to know I'm
wrong
My confidence in her restored, for her, for peace, I
long
I feel so bitter angry, my moods they fluctuate
I cannot think of anything else, I can't quite
calculate
I can't control my temper, my outburst, a big
surprise!
But I know it when I see her friends; I can see it in
their eyes
She comes to help to calm me down; she's been
missing for a while
She takes my face in close to hers, then says with
worried smile
"I don't know what's got into you; you used to be
my rock"
Its then that all my fears ring true, his seed clings
to her frock!!

By Dermot Nelson, 2010

MIND WANDERINGS

Sometimes my mind wanders to places in my past
I imagine people who aren't here, friendships I
thought would last!
With some, just seemed to drift apart, out of sight
and out of mind
But others ended bitterly, through fights, and
words unkind!
Then there are the people, who no longer draw a
breath
Taken to the Lord, our God, by sad untimely
death.
I begin to wonder why, why I didn't stay in touch.
With people who, for many years, seemed to mean
so much
And with all the people that I can no longer call a
friend
Are the problems that we have so big, they're
problems we can't mend!
The fights they all seem petty when I think of
friends passed on
The ones you'll never see to speak too, because
they've already come and gone

And when I'm drunk and haven't slept, emotion's
running high
These are the friends that I recall, the ones for
whom I cry!

By Dermot Nelson, 2010

THE WEEKLY ROUTINE

Monday starts with stomach pain,
And Toilet calls; Not Again!

Tuesday still not feeling great
And every week I get up late.
I look back with woeful sorrow
When I think of all I spent and borrowed

Wednesday morn is not too bad,
By eve feel better, and so I'm glad.

By Thursday noon, developed a thirst.
By Thursday night must quench or burst.

Friday noon though always tired,
The thoughts of pub I do admire.
I imagine all that I could miss,
If I fail to go out on the piss.
All my friends who I'd see there,
Lovely girls, and what they'd wear.
I begin to feel exhilaration
About that evening's destination.
I go home, shower, shave and... DRESS.
The plan: NOT TO GET IN A MESS!
Once in the pub I start off slow
But gradually increase the flow.
It's all a laugh and music's good.
"WOULD YOU HAVE A SHOT?" "I WOULD, I WOULD!"

My plan has gotten complicated,
As I find myself inebriated.
I go back to a stranger's party,
Hoping for a girl that's tarty
But as per usual, it's mostly boys,
Shouting, singing, just drunken noise

I wake up feeling slightly odd,
And wander home on my todd.
I get some sleep and now feel fresh
For lends of money; my mum I press.
I have some food; a bit to eat,
Make sure my clothes are nice and neat.
And when all dressed and had the grub:
Once more it's time to hit the pub!
Tonight there seems a lot more out;
Friendly faces all about.
Whilst drinking vodka and red bull,
I decide it's time to pull.
I find myself in conversation
Which leads to one clear declaration!
She has a need or wants to dance;
A night club down the road we'll chance.
Another hour, lots to drink,
I'm beginning to be in a kink.
I'm starting to feel, I'm in the mood
To get her home MUST NOT BE RUDE!
She wants to wait until the end,
As though I don't mind I must pretend.
I have another great big drink

And further into drunk I sink.
Night clubs over, it's time to go.
I'm stumbling, falling, walking slow,
She gets me home and says GOODNIGHT!
"NEXT WEEKEND? …. MEET?" "WE MIGHT!"
I see my mother's exasperation
When she sees her son's intoxication.
I try and talk; converse so deep
But end up falling in a heap.

Sunday afternoon, I wake.
I don't feel good, there's no mistake.
I remember things I've said and done,
Silly yarns I said and spun,
My stomach sick, and a headache,
That seems to make the whole room quake.
I rise, I wash, don't want to eat,
But this hangover, I must beat.
I hit the pub, I get the cure
And within an hour I'm fit for more.
Tonight I'm going to drink quite slow
While over thoughts of mine, I'll mow.
After hours of careful thinking
And quiet anti-social drinking
I've come up with one simple conclusion
Of which I'm under no illusion
That excited drunken anticipation
Has led to chronic masturbation.

By Dermot Nelson, 2009

The Whistler

The whistler played on the city streets
A kinder face one rarely meets
He played so well by the Ulster hall
But to a bottles bottom he was prone to fall

Some talent you had with board and note
And over you your friends would dote
Your gifts with them you would share
And for your well-being these friends did care

A life so fragile needs one more start
Through all his flaws still full of heart
A kind soul who had gotten lost
Life is cheap but at great cost

While at a New-lodge tower steep
The reaper knows a soul he'll reap
As the devils work makes humans twisted
A man takes a blade and to another lifts it

But the devil has not won this fight
For to take this soul he has no right
Now the musician on the street won't roam
But our Lord God takes an Angel home

Now the music's no longer on our street
With no more whistler to smile or greet
Goodbye fair whistler with your happy face
Now play your tunes in a better place

(In Memory of Dee Core, one of Belfast's skater/buskers) By Dermot Nelson, 2012

For a friend passed on

While looking at the sky I'm thinking of another

It was days like this I spent with you my brother

We'd cause some trouble and have to run

Or just chill and relax while lying in the sun

I know I left, and things turned bad

Wrapped up in me and always sad

Not coming home consumed by fear

Maybe I should have at least been near

Why'd you have to go so young?

Another victim, by narcotics stung

With heads all warped we go insane

And the ripples are our loved ones pain

Even with our great big mess

They pray for us, our souls they bless

I didn't make your funeral

But on days like this I see you pal!

By Dermot Nelson, 2008

It was like a dream

Behind my back my arms they twist
And they close the cuffs around my wrists
What's happening, no this can't be real
What's happened, it's a botched drug deal
My mind is racing though I'm in shock
Time now slows to drawn out tick-tocks
My senses now they all seem heightened
My burden now cannot be lightened
I see my parents I see their faces
As my mind takes me to desperate places
My whole world has turned upside down
For want of a buzz, want of a pound
Why has this happened and why now
My heart speeds up but time slows down
When in the cell it's so surreal
Sick to my stomach I begin to feel
My resolve, I must accept my fate
Stand and be judged at a later date
How did I get in this mess?
Sleeps now disturbed by regret and stress
I don't dare pray or ask for help
For I broke oath before when a good hand dealt
I just stew in nervous fear
Each day more as my court date draws near
When finally the court day has come
I feel relief before it's begun
For closure I long more and more
Now I pray, not a cell door!

By Dermot Nelson, 2011

My Season's Greetings

To drunken louts about the town
To tired people coming down
To all those who are Christmas grouches
To those opening presents on their couches
To those who fill us with Christmas cheer
To those who bring the Christmas beer
To kids eating lots of sweats
And those sharing out their Christmas treats
To all of those with a sick belly
To those watching Christmas shows on telly
To those having turkey and having ham
Or even simple bread and jam
I hope you all enjoy your day
And tomorrow all come out to play!!

By Dermot Nelson, 2012

Thug like heroes

Such epic heroes both tough and strong
With both might and arrogance they're rarely
wrong
Through intimidation imposing rule
School yard bullies long out of school
The world, they think, owes them respect
And women's lust they expect
Each time they drink they show off their might
But they are able, and so have right?
Fight each other leave us alone
Don't threaten us with hostile tones
You're just bullies or can't you see
You can shut me up but my pen I'm free

By Dermot Nelson, 2012

For My Buddy

To my buddy who is in such pain, somehow you're just
not the same

You drink all day and take diazepam, a shadow of your
former man

Drink and drugs, your confidence steal, changing your
perception of what's really real

Just being your friend fills me with pride, I wish I could
help how you feel inside

Remember who you are and where you're from;
remember just how far you have come

You fought every knock, got on your feet; don't be a
legend that's so young beat

You used to laugh more, and smile, but now it only lasts
a while

You mean so much to your friends and me, if only you
seen what we see

Don't give up, don't get lost, think of what you'll lose,
think of the cost

There's so much left that you can give, with pride and
power you should live

The future for you, can be so bright; I see your name in
shinning lights

So come back brother and beat this trial, make the world
laugh and make me smile.

By Dermot Nelson, 2012

It's funny, I Love you

It's funny, when I think of how it started, you were my
best friend

Never knowing that to each other, one day our hearts
we'd lend

Summer days we spent together, joking in the sun

Splashing in the river shallows, just us together having
fun

Lying on the bank, waiting for cloths to dry

Looking at the clouds above, on soft grass we both
would lie

They were such perfect days, for which my thanks is
due

I should have realised then, that I'd fall in love with you

It's funny, all we'd known before, all our fears and pain

When together they seemed to drift away and not come
back again

In autumn it turned cold out, and I had to move away

You used to seem so tough, but you cried on my leaving
day

I was only gone a month, when you followed to say you
care

That night was our first nights love, of all the love we'd
share

Our first night it was so perfect and for that my thanks
is due

For that's the night I realised, you loved me and I loved
you

It's funny; it can fill you with new patience, reverence and concern

When you feel that you are truly loved, a love that you return

With that winter came Our Christmas, although we both went home

It was only for a visit, for we'd found a place to call our own

And though our place was small, it was for us a brand new start

Our home we shared together will be forever in my heart

For the love we shared inside those walls, I feel that thanks is due

I think it's there I realised, that forever I'd love you

It's funny, tragic occurrences happen often but you think won't happen you

And finally when a tragedy strikes you can't believe it's true

After winter it got warmer, as it became the spring

You began to feel unwell, and I bought you a ring

I got down on one knee, and asked you to be my wife

You wept as you said yes, but it was you who'd fulfilled my life

For the time once we were married, I know that thanks is due

I just wish that I had had more time, to show you I love you. **(By Dermot Nelson, 2012)**

Stupid Games

My patience is getting sorely tested

As my efforts are being constantly bested

Again and again she shows her skill

This game for me now holds no thrill

It shouldn't be so complicated

I'm getting worse, I'm so frustrated

She gloats and rubs it in my face

Why can't I put her in her place?

My niece's game is off the chart

THAT'S IT! I'm sick of stupid Mario-cart!!

(For my Niece Amy Louise Nelson, with love from Uncle Dermot, 2012)

Still paying......

Broken by your absence, I lay crying on a floor

Trying to hide my grief, behind my bedroom door

In desperation praying for God to make you mine

Weighing up all my sins, feeling punished for my crimes

It seemed that punishment though, was particularly cruel

As you crushed me at my weakest, and you broke unwritten rules

In such a weakened state, you took my dignity and pride

You belittled me and made squirm and tortured me inside

But even worse than that, you bruised and pricked my heart

And though my life began again, something's could not restart

If I ever think of you, I still feel a sense of loss

And I also become aware again, of how losing you still costs

But I suppose that I should thank you, as now I'm feeling tough

After spending so long feeling weak, wondering 'Why wasn't I enough?'

And now though I have confidence it's riddled with mistrust

Meaning every time someone gets close I end things unjust

I spent so long hurting; I was pathetic, depressed and sad

Then spent another lifetime angry, bitter, drunk and feeling bad

And although I love my life now, I feel there's something lacking

The thought that I can't love again, sometimes gets so distracting

I want a time to come where I am finally free

I want a time to come when I can allow someone to love me

Maybe loves just something that's chemically induced

Maybe it's just some internal trick, to help our species bond or reproduce

But if that's true, why is it that it that carries such weight and pain

And if it's not, why is it that even after hurt, we can play it like a game

Maybe it is that love isn't really real

Or maybe it is but through hurt it's robbed, or numbed till we can't feel.

By Dermot Nelson, 2012

Aggravated, Aggressive, Righteousness

A fool utters more stupid lies, and twists
what's known is true,

He convinces himself even, and then
complains when what's due is due,

But we no longer suffer fools; he should try
and make amends

Our patience has mockingly been tested; we'll
no longer play pretend

And if the righteous doubt his words, if he
utters more untruth,

Then for each and every insult counted, the
hand of justice collects a tooth!

By Dermot Nelson, 2012

Past, Present and Future

Looking back to days of my infliction, a personal, painful, crucifixion

It all seems now like a distant dream; no more visions come in painful streams

With recovery I felt such tolerance, but NOW, no time for false pretence

No time for peoples sordid lies, no time for the boy with his wolf cries

Now feeling strong were once felt weak, I now have pride were once was meek

The world for me is looking up, though so easily life can be corrupt

With calm and caution I'll steer my course, I won't be swayed by negative force

I'll be the best, an honest prediction, and I'll stay strong with my conviction

I won't falter and get sucked in, not this time, this time I win.

By Dermot Nelson, 2012

SEA SHELLS/LIFE IN IRELAND

SHE sells sea shells on the sea shore,
While SHE marries for money, a working class
whore,
HE swallows all of his pride and sells door to door
While HE takes all a poor man has and still he
wants some more,

SHE wanders home to her kids, and thinks 'I feel
so old'
While SHE doesn't realise, her marriage is all but
cold
HE picks himself up from broken down, shaken by
the man
While to evict another number HE has a sordid
plan

Now getting on and humbled, SHE'S led an honest
but hard life
Replaced now by another, SHE knows she was a
trophy wife
An honest though a tiresome life has not hardened
an HONEST MAN
But it angers him now to hear, the RICH MAN lie
upon the stand.

By Dermot Nelson, 2012

The Best Day Ever

My happiest day up until then was the day I'd met
my wife.
It never crossed my mind that you'd come into my
life

As soon as I'd laid eyes on you, it was love at first
sight
I thought 'I'll guide you through each day, and
keep you safe through every night'

When holding you in my arms I felt MY life had
just begun
As though the world had given me something
special, something precious, I felt I'd won

I felt so overwhelmed, as our hearts, they beat in
tune
With slow and single tears of joy I promised you
the earth, the sun and moon

And to you I made a sacred oath to provide love
and protection
And again my breath was taken away, as I gazed
upon perfection

And when you gripped my little finger my feelings
I could not contain
My eyes outburst in flowing tears as my heart then
ruled my brain

And all of creation made sense to me as you
gripped my hand again
For nature and miracle combined can break the
hearts of men

I was told feelings would be so strong when it
would be my turn
But nothing had prepared me for the day my child
was born.

**(Inspired by my sister Maria talking about having
children, all my love Dermot,2012)**

I'm here

Sometimes it seems you're ruled by fear, afraid to
let another near
Doubt and despair both have you crushed, is it
now so hard for you to trust
Sometimes I wish you would just cry, take down
your wall, don't live a lie
Its seems as though your Spirits shaken, and deep
inside your heart is breaking

Let me in, let me take your hand, I'll share your
pain, I'll understand
And if I can't, I'll still be near, for if you need me, I
will be right here

Sometimes you're lost, and so alone, in quiet pain,
without sigh or groan
You've been through so very much; it's hard to tell
if you're weak or tough
Sometimes you look so melancholy, afraid to live,
but this folly
Its seems as though all your Spirits gone, to a
distant past your heart belongs

Let me in, let me hold you tight, I'll keep you safe
through day and night
And if you still can't let me near, then I'll wait for
you, I'll wait right here

Sometimes you seem stuck in the past, afraid to love in-case it won't last
You're independence is both weak and strong, it's to my heart though that you belong
I roar inside the things I feel, as our time together our silence steals
Its seems as though some kindred hearts are destined to be torn apart

Let me in, let me ease your pain, I'll take care of you, our lives can change
And if you feel sad, confused, or fear, I won't be far, I'll be right here

Some people think that they are cursed; they seem to suffer worse and worse
Eventually can't take anymore, they turn off lights, they close the door
But you don't need to feel this way; I can help you find the light of day
And I will show you to a happy place, for I long to see your happy face

I wish I could have taken your bane, held you, helped you ease your pain
I couldn't help, though was so near, now in quiet pain I linger here.

By Dermot Nelson, 2012

THE DARKNESS FADES

In a world of violence we co-exist, in a world of
cloud and smoke and mist,
There are cries and shrieks of pain, families, lives
all torn and maimed
But in the darkness there is a light, a place of peace
and quiet nights
And when you find this place of bright, it's like
you once were blind now blessed with sight
After so long being deaf and in the dark, you now
see the morn and hear the lark
And you are free, you realise you've choice, your
heart and soul combined rejoice
A renewed life for you begins; you forgive yourself
of all your sins
But you must recall and not forget, the life you've
led, the burdens met
You must remember how you landed here, and
recognise those still ruled by fear
And even though they can cause you stress,
remember, you were once in this mess
Be kind to those still afraid, for a penance they've
already paid
For your kindness can help to ease the pain, for
those whose world is still insane
And if you can help those souls you meet, then
maybe they'll find a place of peace
The darkness fades, the light is strong, it's to
happiness that we all belong.

By Dermot Nelson, 2012

Written in a variety of styles 'These things I imagine' boasts different writings for the whole family to enjoy. It is a journey through the life and the imagination of the author, Dermot Nelson.

With the first section devoted to plays he gives us a first-hand insight into the world of drugs and sectarianism in certain parts of Ireland.

Set in Dublin's inner-city and suburbs, 'Changes, Through Their Eyes' is made up of seven interlinking monologues based on the ripple effects of drugs and addiction. It has both comical and hard hitting elements and over the course of the piece we see how people's mind-sets and opinions change as they themselves are directly or indirectly affected by drugs or addiction.

'In The Clear' tells a tale of a young man's battle with his conscience and his own perception of right and wrong. Set in Northern Ireland, the troubles are supposedly coming to an end, but there are some who refuse to let that happen. As Adam folds under the pressure of his peers, he allows pack mentality to take control, with horrific consequences. Now haunted by his by his alter ego and overcome with guilt, he begins to question whether this really is the pack he belongs to.

After our trip to Ireland, the mood is quickly changed as Nelson takes us deep into the darkest most gothic realms of his imagination.

'Rabu' is an epic tale detailing one man's transformation from a selfless young peasant

fending for his family, to a ruthless stalker of the night, hunting to satisfy his relentless bloodlust. The story heralds the crumbling of mortals against the will of the abiding. Dark and poetic 'Rabu' symbolises the power of an undying evil. Written in rhythmic style, Nelson has created his own style of writing which is said to have similarities to works of both Shakespeare and Edgar Allen Poe.

With his last play in this collection, Nelson invites us on a trip to the North Pole.

'When Santa Turned Bad' is a comical, light hearted Christmas adventure with jokes for the whole family to enjoy. Charming and worthy of a good chuckle, this play boasts a range of characters from a clumsy Father Christmas to a busy-body Mrs Clause, from an interfering Mother in Law to a Naughty Niggling Nymph and finally from a chorus of Giddy Elves to the most Unlikely of Heroes.

Nelson begins the second section of the book, with two poems aimed at children. Though both poems are colourful and fun and written for children's enjoyment, 'The Naughty Puppy' also encompasses some educational messages.

After which, using both comical and dramatic elements, Nelson explores some of life's most joyous and sorrowful events. He, in some depth, catalogues through verse, some experiences which many of us have or will encounter, and thus his poems have a resonating impact. Boasting realistic themes such as (vivid dreams) (loving relationships, breakups and betrayal) (the lingering pain from the death of friends or loved) (abuse of alcohol, drugs or people) (inequality and different aspects of society) (and finally, children's games, childbirth, and marriage) collectively these poems make one expressive and enthralling read.

Dermot Nelson was born in Kilmainham, Kells, County Meath, Ireland in 1983. Coming from a family of eleven children he always loved to hear stories from and share stories with, his parents, siblings and friends alike. At the age of eleven he was jestingly giving the title of a 'bull-shitter' by his friends at school. This however didn't deter him from his love of story-telling and as a teenager he began forming his tall-tales into poem and essay form. However, during a stint with drugs as a young adult Nelson lost all of his early writings and his creativeness seemed to be stifled. Upon his completing his recovery in his late twenties he then attended a 16 week cross-border community course with Springboard Opportunities Limited, Belfast. It was there while attending Springboards Performance and Community based workshops that he once again began to wield a pen, and hasn't stopped since. On completion of his course with Springboard Nelson applied to Belfast Metropolitan College, Tower Street, and was awarded a place to study for two years, for a Higher National Diploma in Performance (Acting). Having achieved his HND in the summer of 2012, he then secured a place at Edinburgh Napier University and Queen Margaret University Edinburgh. He is currently studying for BA Honours Degree in Acting for Stage and Screen and is due to graduate in June 2014. *These Things I Imagine* is his first publication, and he is adamant that it will be the first of many.